One Hundred and One Patchwork Patterns

Quilt Name Stories, Cutting Designs, Material Suggestions,
Yardage Estimates, Definite Instructions for
Every Step of Quilt Making

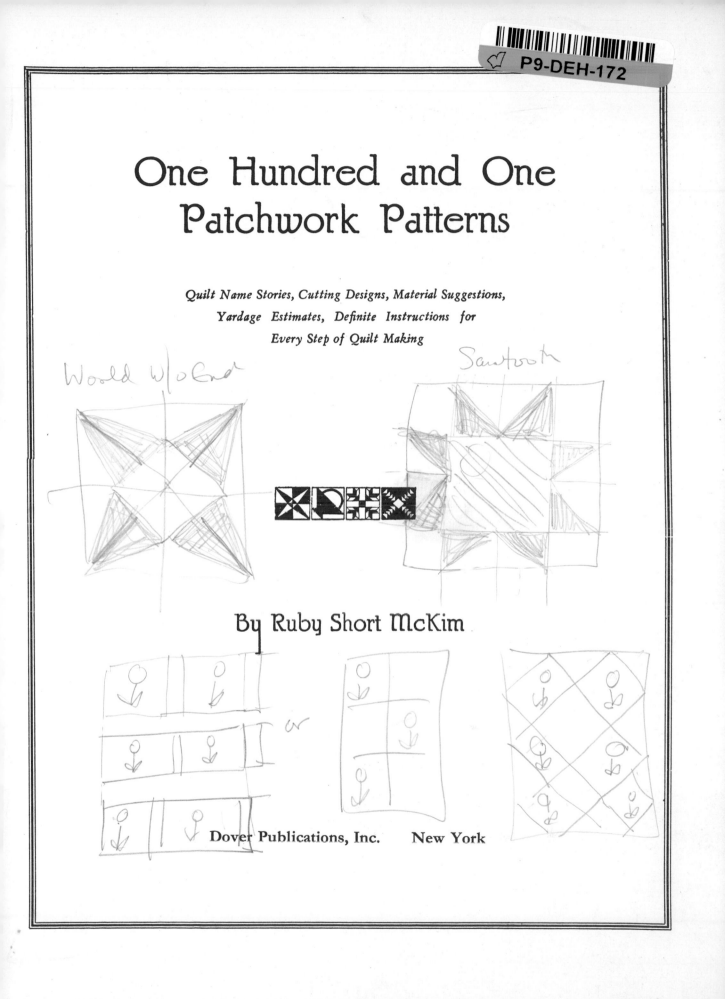

By Ruby Short McKim

Dover Publications, Inc.   New York

Published in Canada by General Publishing Company, Ltd., 30 Lesmill Road, Don Mills, Toronto, Ontario.
Published in the United Kingdom by Constable and Company, Ltd., 10 Orange Street, London WC 2.

This Dover edition, first published in 1962, is a revised version of the work originally published by McKim Studios in 1931.

Standard Book Number: 486-20773-0
Library of Congress Catalog Card Number: 63-1453

Manufactured in the United States of America
Dover Publications, Inc.
180 Varick Street
New York, N. Y. 10014

TABLE OF CONTENTS

INDEX TO CUTTING PATTERNS

INTRODUCTION

HANDCRAFTS, like all phases of human endeavor, rather run in varying cycles. Some of us were born in the Pyrography period and reared on hand painted plates with much beshaded backgrounds; others of us date back to the stork painted on velvet with a pressed pen technique, while all of mature age have survived the era of crochet boudoir caps, of tinfoil and glass paintings, and much be-beaded lamp shades!

True, there have ever been crafts worth while, some arts where beauty combined with purpose to create the "joys forever." Our treasure chests contain exquisitely fashioned needlework on garments, household linens and purely decorative pieces. There is hand-made lace of such dignity and daintiness that it is sheer beauty, whenever used. There have been scattered gems of weaving, batik, pottery, and metal work, of basketry, woodcarving, tooled leather, decorative painting, and such for countless generations. Tradition tells us that after primitive man first shaped for use his rude bowls and jars, he very soon daubed them with crimson clay and purple berry juice—to add beauty.

We have devised an hundred ways to fabricate floor coverings, draperies, and bedding. Which brings us to quilts and the no end of fascinating patterns and tales in their history. Through all the changing fads of woven bead-belts or melon seed portieres our quilts have been always with us. A wholesome thing it is, too, that American women have so saved and planned and pieced. To have wrought beauty even from beautiful surroundings has not always been achieved; but to salvage beauty and usefulness from coarse waste materials was the everyday accomplishment of our pioneer mothers who hooked rugs and pieced quilts.

Some way we are apt to think of the quilt makers as mature or even old, but a second thought assures us they were often merely girls. Pioneer movements are not sponsored by those who have passed life's meridian. It takes youth, with its unspoiled imaginings to blaze trails, to leave the family hearth for the open road, to hazard security for chance. So most of the families who surged their way westward were young as the civilization which they were formulating. A girl-wife, driving an ox team, with her firstborn held close in her strong young arms or under her stronger young heart, was the heroine of the day. Not that they called her a heroine then; no; but her timid sister who stayed with "pa and ma" back in York State or Ca'lina may have spent the rest of her spinster days in envying willful Emily who rode away with John.

And the story of their wanderings, their few original possessions, their accumulations, the friendships formed, their abiding faith and the home established, is the story of patchwork quilts. Study the names of patterns and again you will know they were so christened by young ladies of imagination, sometimes devout, sometimes droll but always kindled by that divine spark of originality. Listen to this for a less-than-500-word history, all quilt names stitched in bed coverlets, which are more comforting, if not more enduring, than words graven in stone:

"London Roads, Ocean Wave, Lost Ship, Star and Compass; Charter Oak, Lafayette Orange Peel, Tail of Benjamin's Kite; Turkey Tracks, Bear's Paw, Indian Hatchet; Washington Pavement and Washington's Plumes; Dolly Madison Block, Whig Rose, Democrat Rose, Philadelphia Beauty, Virginia Star, Georgetown Circle; Horn of Plenty —Hovering Hawks! Mill Wheel, Churn Dash, Tea Leaves, Anvil, Brown Goose, Chips and Whetstones, Clamshell, Corn and Beans, the Log Cabin, Arrowheads. The Pine Tree and the Little Beech, Folded Love Letter, Swing-in-the-Center, Eight Hands 'Round'; Free Trade Block, 54-40 or Fight, Tippecanoe and Tyler Too, Clay's Choice, Little Giant, Mexican Rose, Lincoln's Platform. The North Wind, Hosanna, World without End, Delectable Mountains, Rose of Sharon, Wagon Tracks, Road to California, Snake Fence, Love Apple, Arkansas Traveler, Oklahoma Boomer, Kansas Troubles, Cactus Basket, Prairie Queen, Texas Treasure, Rising Sun, World's Fair, Mrs. Cleveland's Choice, Coxey's Camp, The Pickle Dish, and Cake Stand, Fanny's Fan, Pullman Puzzle— Hour Glass!"

We have not shown them all, only a hundred or so of them are contained in our pages, but we have found bits of interesting history about these and drafted patterns from which you can copy them. We have estimated the yardage, suggested ways of setting blocks together into tops and planned suitable quilting designs.

During years of experience there have been questions come to us concerning every phase of quilt making. We have tried to answer them all in this book, to tell you every practical, helpful angle in the game of quilt making.

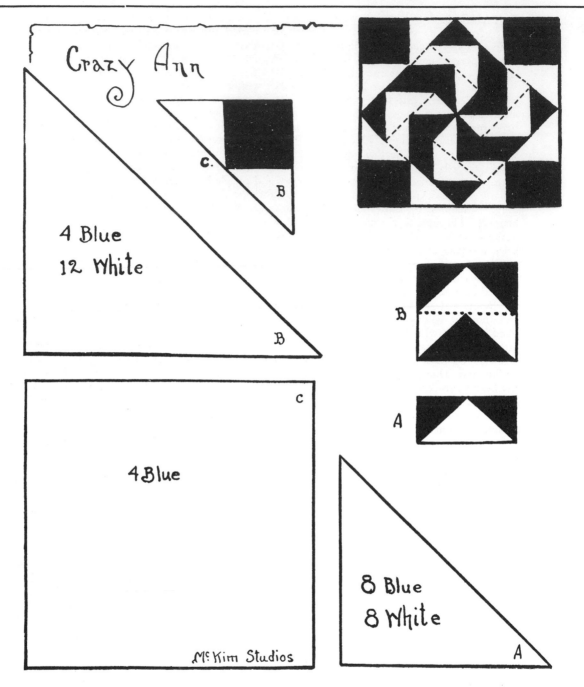

Crazy Ann

c.

B

4 Blue
12 White

B

B

A

c

4 Blue

McKim Studios

8 Blue
8 White

A

CRAZY ANN

CRAZY ANN is a quilt that can be done on the sewing machine as it is all straight seam sewing. If you cut the pieces all a seam larger and sew back to the unit sizes above, a block will finish 12 inches square. Its complex appearance unravels very simply—first piece an oblong A and another with colors reversed. Join them to form B, then join four squares B to make the swastika center to which four triangles C are added. Only one caution; the four pieced squares must go together in identical sequence in all of the blocks. If the whirl-like movement reverses in some, they will never set together properly.

This is one of the quilts so well beloved that we chose it to offer you. The Swastika-like motive comes in light blue with the four corner squares a medium blue, remainder of block and alternate plain squares white. Of course any colors may be used if you cut them yourself from a pattern, but the two blues with white always make an excellent combination.

Material Estimate: 42 blocks — 21 pieced and 21 plain — requires: 1¾ yards light blue, 6 yards white, 1½ yards medium blue—9¼ yards complete.

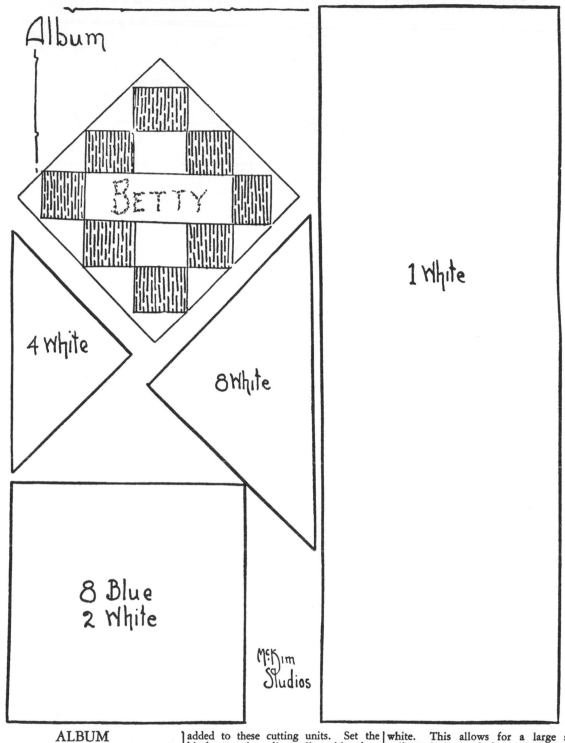

Album

BETTY

1 White

4 White

8 White

8 Blue
2 White

McKim
Studios

ALBUM

THE ALBUM quilt is a real old-timer. Its original purpose was for a gift for a bride-to-be. A group of friends would get together and each would piece a block and embroider her name upon it!

One block when completed is ten and one-half inches square if seams are added to these cutting units. Set the blocks together diagonally with alternate white squares measuring ten and one-half inches. The total number of pieced and white blocks used of course varies according to the size and shape of the quilt desired.

Material Estimate: Blocks 10½ inches square, 15 inches on the diagonal, require 2 yards of blue and 6 yards of white. This allows for a large size quilt 79 inches wide by 85 inches long. This would be five blocks long and 5 wide, diagonally placed, plus a 5-inch border of white at top and bottom and 2-inch border of white at sides. All together there are 25 pieced blocks, 16 plain blocks, 16 plain ½ blocks, diagonally cut, and 4 plain ¼ blocks on four corners.

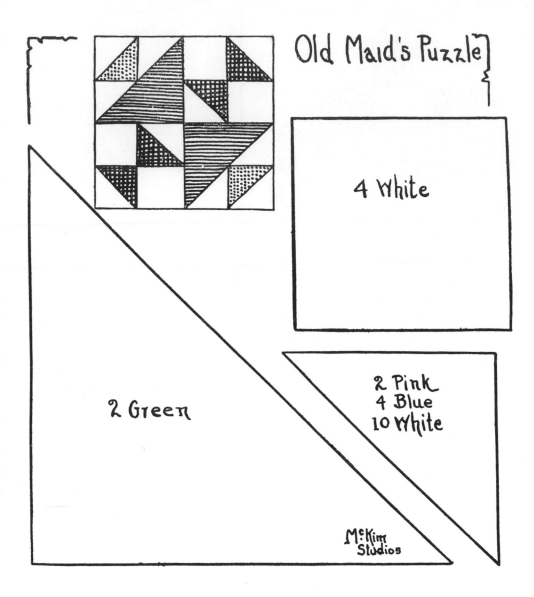

OLD MAID'S PUZZLE

ONE MAY be certain that "Old Maid's Puzzle" is a genuine antique, because there haven't been any "old maids" in a generation, and "bachelor girls" are not so easily puzzled!

The triangles and square here given are exact size of the finished parts in a block 9 inches square. Cut cardboard patterns from these. Trace around them onto material and cut a seam larger. This is really quite a simple block to piece, four squares of two varieties. The color scheme suggested uses odd scraps of pink, blue, and green prints with white set together checkerboard style with alternate plain blocks, each color forming a pattern in diagonals across the whole quilt.

The "hour glass" quarter of this block repeated into a strip makes an attractive pieced border.

Material Estimate: 72 blocks, 36 pieced and 36 plain, 8 blocks wide by 9 long and a 5-inch border all around will make a quilt 82 by 98 inches. It requires ½ yard pink, 1 yard blue, 1½ yards green, and 6 yards white, a total of 9 yards.

A geometric Tulip design or four flowers would quilt nicely on the alternate plain squares.

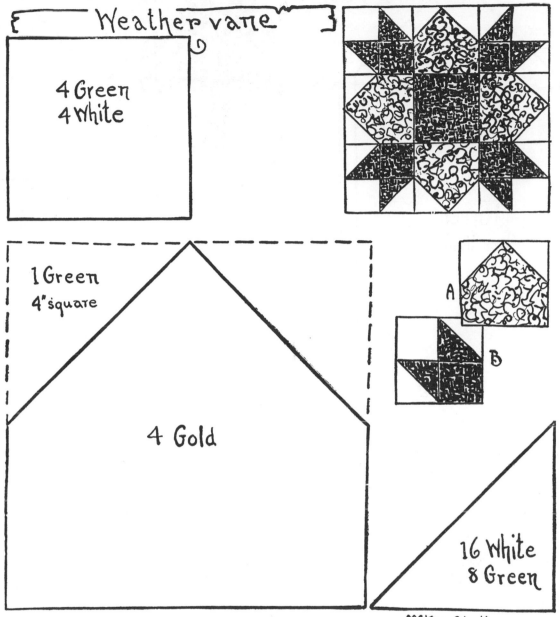

McKim Studios.

WEATHERVANE

THIS patchwork pattern is called the Weathervane, and dates back to the time when great-grandmother used that commodity to "calc'late a change," instead of listening to a scientific forecast on the radio. But her pattern, the weathervane, is one of the loveliest of our old-time quilt designs.

Cardboard patterns may be cut exact size from the units here given, the four-inch center square and three other shapes used. Trace around these with a lead-pencil onto your material and then cut a seam larger all around so the finished block will be 12 inches square.

It makes up very simply; small green and white triangles sew into 8 squares which combine with a green and a white square to make the four corner blocks. White triangles on the gold form four other blocks, then they all set together as shown to form the weathervane. This is a charming pattern for a quilted pillow of silk scraps or calico; as well as for an entire quilt.

The quilt finishes 72 by 84 inches and includes 6 by 7 blocks, 21 pieced blocks and 21 plain. It sets together with alternate plain 12-inch squares and requires 2 yards of green, 2 yards of gold (this allows for binding), and 4½ yards white.

Pine Tree

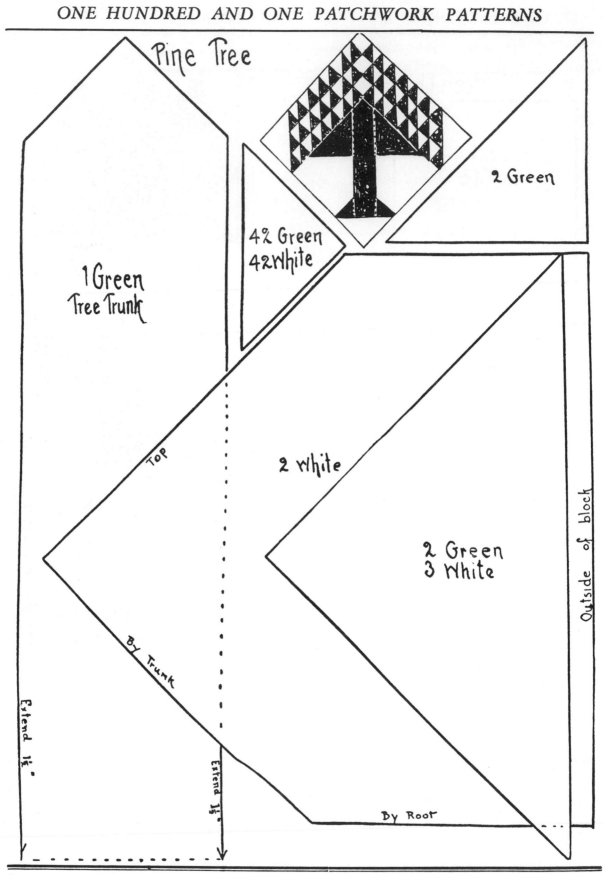

2 Green

4% Green
42 White

1 Green
Tree Trunk

TOP

By Trunk

2 White

2 Green
3 White

Outside of block

Extend 1½"

Extend 1½"

By Root

PINE TREE

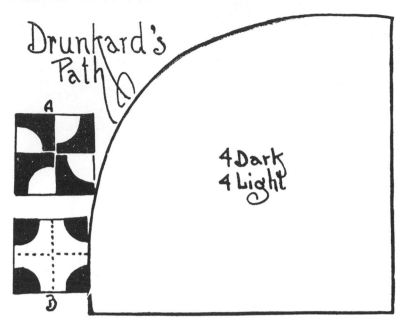

THE PINE TREE blocks make a very handsome quilt. It takes sixteen pieced blocks to make a quilt about eighty-four inches square, aside from its border. These blocks must set together diagonally with alternating blocks of white, cut the exact size of the pieced block. The cardboard patterns are the exact size in which the pieces should be cut. The size of one block when put together is about fifteen inches. Extend tree trunk three inches longer than pattern given.

Lay the cardboard patterns on the material. Trace around with pencil carefully; cut a seam larger, sewing on the pencil line. The two white pieces of irregular shape have to be fitted in as marked on the edges; aside from this, the "Pine Tree" is largely a business of sewing small triangles into squares and adding them together. Allow 6½ yards of white and 4½ yards of green. This sounds like a lot of material, but the smaller the pieces the larger the yardage.

DRUNKARD'S PATH

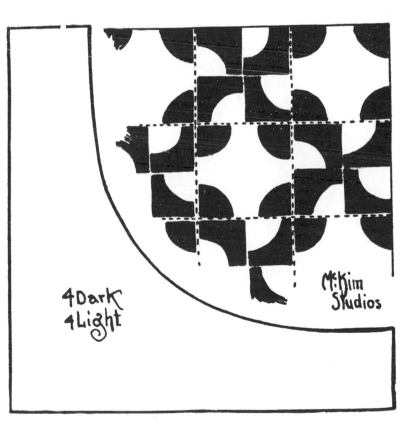

A DRUNKARD'S PATH is easy enough to explain, once the start is made! And this is not a temperance lecture either. It is a set of instructions and cutting patterns for one of the most attractive old-time quilts in the list.

Colors should be sharply contrasted, that is the light really light, and the dark quite dark. Then they piece together into two separate blocks A and B, each 8 inches square, and these set together as shown into any desired size. These do not allow for seams, so cut them ¼ inch larger all around. The light center of B may be cut in one piece instead of four as shown. Borders in strips of both colors used are specially good on a quilt of startling design such as this.

Material Estimate: This quilt takes equal amounts of light and dark, but they do not cut to as perfect advantage as they appear, so would allow 4½ yards of light and 4½ yards of dark. 55 blocks of A, 55 blocks of B, 10 blocks wide by 11 blocks long or 80 inches by 88 inches.

A Maple Leaf or any other Leaf design would quilt nicely on the large white spaces, with a Feather Circle in the large centers.

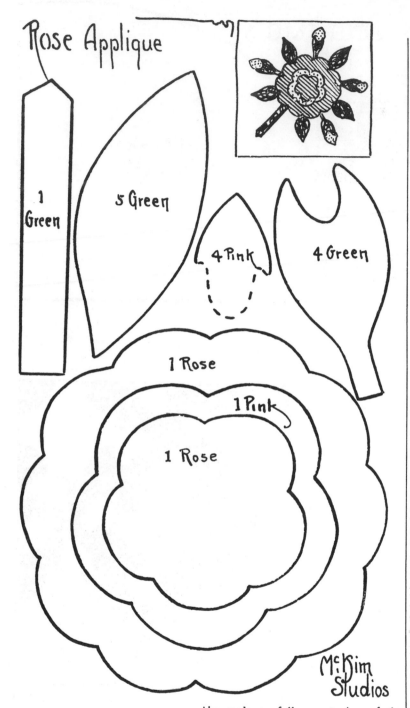

blind stitched onto the block. Fancy stitching does not add to the simple charm of a design like the rose applique. In a built-up rose a row of print between plain tint layers is quaint. Many antique rose quilts alternated turkey red with yellow print calico and surrounded the flower with bottle green leaves for a vividly colorful block.

When setting the top together the Rose Applique will make a better design if the stems lead out to the sides of the quilt, that would make the three left rows place as shown in the sketch above, and the three right hand rows reverse.

Material Estimate: 42 blocks, 21 plain, 21 applique, 5½ yards white, 1 yard rose, 2-3 yard pink, 1½ yards green, total of 8 2-3 yards.

The finished quilt will measure about 72 inches by 84 inches.

V BLOCK

ONE BLOCK of a V quilt has no chance to show the beauty of the design repeated. Blocks are all pieced and placed parallel to the quilt's edges so that one color follows a general vertical pattern and the other crosses in horizontal rows. This makes both a dainty overlay of designs and lovely background areas for quilting.

The V Block is a perfect example of a pattern that gives entirely different effects depending on the way the quilt is "set up." With alternate plain squares, with white or colored strips, with color V's alternating or forming a pattern, each plan would certainly make a different looking quilt.

An especially firm weave cloth must be used for any pattern like this that can not cut on true bias. Small sketch A shows the procedure of piecing a unit which in turn combines with the large white corners and other pieced triangles to form a 12-inch square, that is, if seams are added to the sizes printed here.

Irregular patterns are of course more difficult to complete smoothly than some of the many square and triangle projects.

Material Estimate: 42 blocks, 6 blocks wide by 7 blocks long would finish about 72 by 84 inches without border. For a top of all pieced blocks allow: 6 yards white, 1½ yards each of two colors.

A Spiderweb design would be an excellent choice for quilting where the 4 long white pieces join.

ROSE APPLIQUE

SOMEBODY always wants an applique patchwork and so in very small space here one is. Satine or fine weave gingham is good material to use. The cardboard cutting patterns should be made carefully, exact sizes of the seven here given. These do not allow for seams, so cut a bit larger all around. This creases and bastes back. Sometimes sheet wadding is used under applique patches to give a raised effect. Plain blocks are cut 12 or more inches square. Applique parts are basted and then

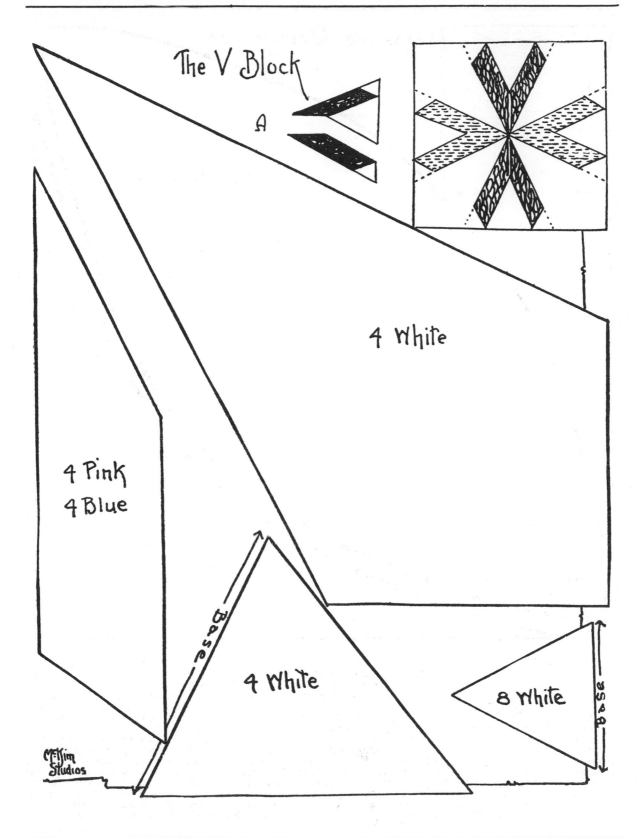

The V Block

A

4 White

4 Pink
4 Blue

Base

4 White

8 White

Base

McKim
Studios

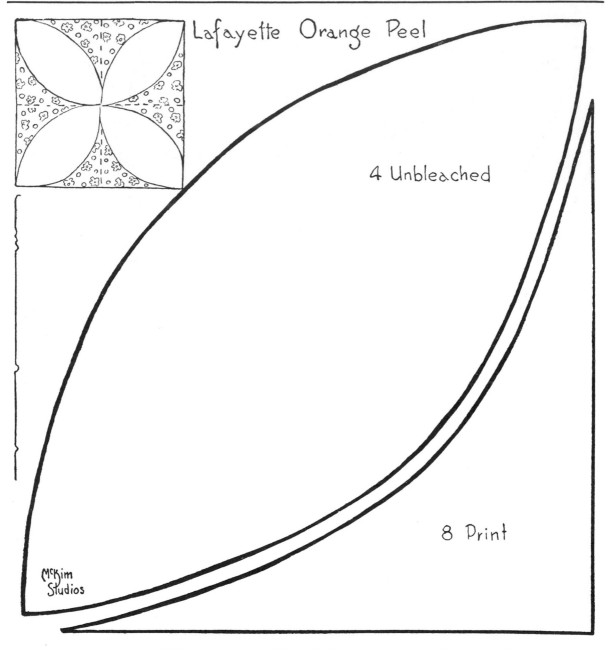

Lafayette Orange Peel

4 Unbleached

8 Print

McKim Studios

LAFAYETTE ORANGE PEEL

YOU may know this block as just the "Orange Peel," but there is such claim to distinction in its heritage that we proudly add the name "Lafayette." The story is that once when the beloved Marquis was feted in Philadelphia, a fair guest at the banquet took home a most beautiful fruit as her souvenir, an orange, imported from Barcelona. To preserve her treasure and the memory of gala days, a pat-tern was carefully made from the pared rind which comes down to us as the Orange Peel quilt block. Some locali-ties call this a "Rob Peter to Pay Paul" which is a sort of general name highly expressive, where the cut part from one section appears to pay the part robbed from another.

The small background pieces marked "print" do not entirely surround the elliptical pieces, but added as shown they form the squares. Each square will be about 6 inches or a block as shown where the four join twelve inches square if a seam is added. This is really daintier and prettier if the pat-tern is small. You might try a sample block without allowing seams extra.

This is one of the all-over plan pat-terns, rather difficult to get all the cor-ners exact but a really lovely quilt when accurately made.

Material Estimate: Allow 5 yards of unbleached and 5 yards of print. This design takes considerable material as it does not cut to a saving. Forty-two blocks put together, 6 blocks wide and 7 blocks long, finishes about 72 by 84 inches. Allow one yard extra for 3-inch border all around if desired.

French Star

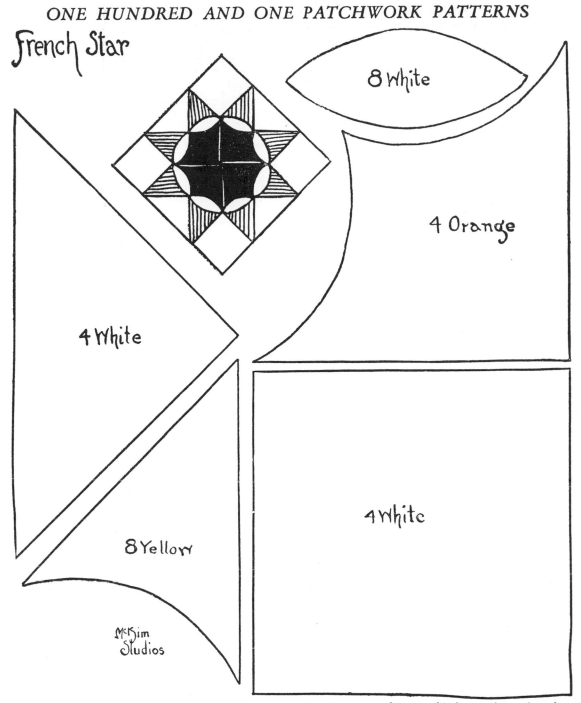

8 White

4 Orange

4 White

4 White

8 Yellow

McKim Studios

FRENCH STAR

NO COLLECTION of quilt block designs is complete without many stars as this symbol was always a favorite.

The French Star is a Canadian pattern varying the eight-pointed star of diamond-shaped blocks by introducing small melon-shaped pieces of the background color or of contrasting hue. These melon-shaped pieces in turn form a wreath and may divide the star into two colors, as rose and pink, two shades of green or orange and yellow as suggested.

In making the French Star, sew two of the cone-shaped pieces to each white triangle, and then sew the corner squares to two of these blocks. The small melon-shaped blocks piece onto the center blocks; these in turn sew into a circle to which are added the oblong blocks and strips which were made first. This takes precise piecing but it makes an unusually attractive design when complete, either for patchwork pillows or for a quilt top. For the quilt, piece the star blocks together, using alternate squares of white of exactly the same size as the pieced blocks and finish with a border of white and color set in strips.

Material Estimate: 11-inch blocks which measure 15½ inches diagonally, may be effectively set together on the diagonal with alternate plain white blocks. 25 pieced blocks with 16 plain blocks, 16 half blocks and 4 quarters, plus a 3-inch border of white at top and bottom only, finishes 78 inches by 84 inches, requiring 6½ yards of white, 1½ yards orange, and 2 yards of yellow.

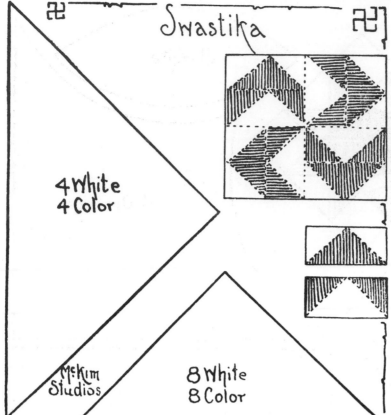

Swastika

4 White
4 Color

McKim
Studios

8 White
8 Color

SWASTIKA

OUR frontier mothers ingeniously converted this ancient symbol of good luck into a quilt pattern which is made simply from two triangles. Sometimes they called it "Flyfoot." The small sketch shows how to make a square which is one-fourth of the complete block. This makes a nine-inch block if seams are added to these triangles. Blocks must all be pieced exactly alike. When they are stacked light must be over light and dark over dark. Otherwise, when set together some would unwind one way, and some another.

Material Estimate: 90 blocks, placed 9 wide and 10 long, make a quilt about 81 by 90 inches. For 45 plain white and 45 pieced blocks allow: 5½ yards white, 3½ yards color.

Pineapples would be effective quilted on the alternate plain blocks, especially if they set diagonally.

PIECED STAR

THERE are many lovely versions of star quilt piecing, varying from four points to eight, and even a feather edged pattern which scintillates with small points along all edges of its large ones. Star blocks have been named for many localities, Northumberland Star, California, St. Louis and Chicago Star, which by the way, is quite different from the "Shooting Star!"

Some are named for people, as "Dolly Madison's Star" and the "Cowboy's Star." There are Morning and Evening versions, falling, flying, rising, rolling, and joining stars, perhaps a hundred varieties of this basic motif.

The one here given is an airy, open-looking block about 11 inches square. It is made by piecing 8 small squares from two triangles each, and four oblong blocks of three triangles each, then sewing them together into the block as shown.

Star blocks may set together with alternate plain squares placed either horizontally or diagonally on the quilt. Here they make a handsome coverlet with white strips about 3 inches wide between blocks joining with a 3-inch square of print at the corners, if seams are added.

Material Estimate: 28 plain blocks, and 28 pieced, 7 wide and 8 long, finishes 77 inches by 88 inches. Allow: 5½ yards white, 3½ yards print.

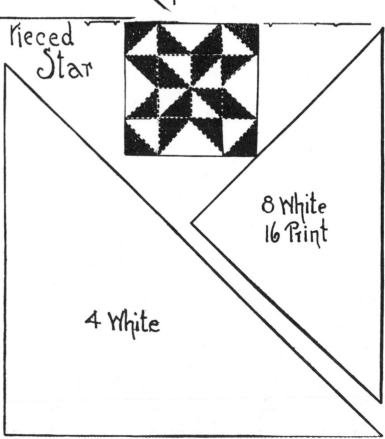

Pieced Star

8 White
16 Print

4 White

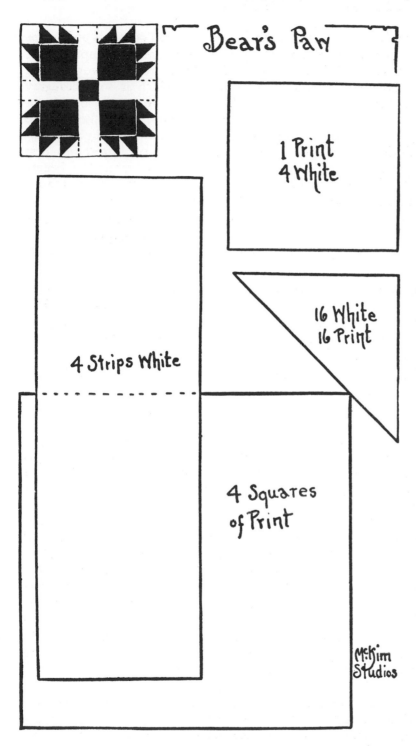

Bear's Paw

1 Print
4 White

16 White
16 Print

4 Strips White

4 Squares
of Print

McKim
Studios

BEAR'S PAW

THE Bear's Paw is unquestionably of frontier origin. Perhaps the pioneer father found such a track in his field or garden one morning and the mother bravely thought "how interesting" instead of "how dangerous." Then we suppose she transferred it to linsey-woolsey or hickory dyed jean, using the unworn parts of much be-patched garments into a sturdy quilt block!

All of our series of old-time quilts have stories, more of them than we can possibly know of course.

This very block, called "Bear's Paw" in certain localities is known as "Duck's Foot in the Mud"! That must have come later, or in more safely settled communities where the bears had moved on out even if paving had not come in.

And the Friends down in Pennsylvania had the very same arrangement in a block called neither "Bear's Paw" nor "Duck's Foot in the Mud," but "Hand of Friendship." From this by curving the angles may have grown another lovely block called "Hands All Around."

A Spiderweb stamped on the alternate plain squares would exactly fit and be harmonious in design, as well as being a very easy pattern to quilt.

This is a simple block to seam. Make each section the size of the given patterns when finished which means allow seams extra.

Material Estimate: Set together with alternate white blocks. These will be about 12½ inches square, depending on the exact size of your pieced "Bear's Paws," 36 blocks, 18 pieced and 18 plain, plus a three-inch border at top and bottom will finish about 72 inches by 79 inches and require 5 yards of white and 3 yards of colored material.

CHOOSE A PATTERN

YOU may be a confirmed "quilt fan" and have a chest full of beautiful coverlets and yet be eager for one more handsome pattern; or you may be just on the verge of attempting your first quilt. At any rate, you surely cannot be indifferent to the charms of patchwork — that simply isn't being done! This wholesome revival of quilt making which is so thoroughly sweeping the country is far more than a fad. One would hardly call Monticello or Mount Vernon "Vogueish." They are the very soul of American art and dignity, and are being more appreciated as such every day. A wing chair, tilt-top table, a four poster, or a highboy may be real Early American or a faithful reproduction. They are the sort of furnishings best loved by the home makers of our land today who appreciate the rich background of beauty and tradition bequeathed to us by Colonial forefathers. The American wing of the Metropolitan Museum is not a fad, and neither, we vouch, is quilt making.

So if you are making a quilt, and it is taking many hours of your time, do not consider them as spent in some fancywork craze such as sealing-wax jewelry one year and painted plaster casts another. You are making a thing of beauty, let us hope—something useful, beautiful and enduring.

Quilts with straight seams such as may be run on the sewing machine are always easiest to make, and by the way, No. 80 thread, machine stitched, gives about as soft a seam as No. 50 hand done. That's a trick worth knowing for the busy woman. Nearly all of the quilts shown do work out in straight seam work. Even such elaborate designs as the Log Cabin, Palm, Zig-Zag or Lone Star sew straight this way.

Others, such as Noonday Lily, Rolling Star, Fish Block, or Sunbeam, have to have a piece fitted in, but this is not so difficult for anyone who sews, and some of the designs are well worth the extra bother.

Some applique quilts are included throughout the book for those who prefer this form of handwork and the lovely effect it gives. Almost always the "Bride's Quilt" was an applique and there are many gorgeous ones in antique collections, bearing testimony of countless hours in their planning, placing and stitchery. We can not show many such in a book of this sort as applique designs are usually so large. For instance, the rose and bud motif of our "Rose Cross" might be used in a Rose of Sharon.

No design has more versions than this same romantic Rose of Sharon—all are the built up rose flower with leaves, buds and stems, but arrangements vary in varying localities, and almost all are lovely. We have patterns on two, a simple and a more elaborate later Rose in special patterns. This was by long odds the most popular "Bride's Quilt" pattern, its significant title coming down from the love songs of Solomon. "I am the Rose of Sharon, and the Lily of the Valleys. As the flower among thorns, so is my love among the daughters. As the apple tree among the trees of the wood, so is my beloved among the sons. My beloved spake, and said unto me, Rise up, my love, my fair one, and come away! For the flowers appear on the earth; the time of the singing of birds is come!" Sounds like a June wedding with roses, valley lilies—or do you think it suggests elopement? To some Colonial girl with imagination it meant a quilt!

But I'm rambling with romance. Getting back to technicalities and patterns there was a difference between the "piece" quilts and "patch" quilts. And, contrary to what you might expect, the patch variety was the aristocrat and the pieced the poor relation. For "patch," sometimes called "sewed on" or "laid work," meant the appliques and required new cloth bought especially, while piecing used every vestige of left-over material, whole parts from worn garments, bits of finery or blanket or tr aded scraps from friends—anything to piece together to make warm covers for the beds.

But "piece" quilts have come up in the world. Such lovely patterns have been evolved from squares, triangles, diamonds, and strips that now women buy handsome materials as some practical husband remarked, "just to cut all up and sew back together!" However, a finished quilt is worth all the price of material and work expended, as well as unsympathetic comment endured. This last is rare; usually we are due for admiration if not envy, from the time the first well-planned block is made until the fine old quilt wears out in service, a generation or two later.

Selecting a design is quite an individual problem and naturally we can not tell you which one you would enjoy most. However, we can tell you which ones are most popular—do you want the one everybody is making or an individual one? There are over a hundred patterns here in your little book, each with possibilities of loveliness. Double Wedding Ring is being made by thousands, usually from the widest possible selection of print scraps. It is unquestionably popular, and yet the owner of an art needlework shop told me recently that in her opinion it was an ugly, erratic design! She had not seen it in our rainbow tint plan which (opinion again!) is really more lovely than when made of all unrelated prints. "Dresden Plate" or "Friendship Ring," the hexagon plan quilts like "Grandmother's Flower Garden" or the "French Bouquet" are favorites and not so because they are easy to make, either. Flower and basket quilts are popular; so are the tree designs and stars—there are some very beautiful star patterns, with the Lone Star best beloved of all.

Irish chains are charming for the amount of work. They come under the class of cut pieces all straight with the weave of the material; no triangles or diamonds to an Irish Chain, but exactly even squares placed as shown with our pattern of Triple Irish Chain or of Double Irish Cross. An ordinary nine-patch set together with alternate plain squares is sometimes called Single Irish Chain, while 9 each way in one block with 3 appliqued onto alternate square corners is called "Forty Niner" and not Quadruple Irish!

Names often have much to do with a quilt's popularity. They do more than identify a certain combination of pieces—a catchy name like Crazy Ann, Dove in the Window, or Wild Goose Chase whets the imagination. We get many letters from people saying, "I have an old family quilt, pieced like the sketch with red, etc., etc., please, what is its name?" And if we can trace back its family branches, the grateful owner feels like the treasure of her ancestors has been made legitimate.

Names of the same pattern do vary. Period, locality and general human contrariness have caused many a fog over quilt escutcheons. An editor of the Chicago Daily News wrote: "Tell me, is it possible that there be various 'Roads to California' with one of them looking like 'Jacob's Ladder' or possibly 'Stepping Stones'?" Yes, and "Drunkard's Path" was sometimes "Wonder of the World," and that long before prohibition, too!

Some quilt names are of pioneer ancestry with a breath of dare and danger like "Bear's Paw," "Crossed Canoes," "Indian Trail," "Prairie Queen." Others have a staid and homey background—"Rail Fence," "Mill Wheel," "Meadow Lily," "Sun Dial," while yet another group bespeaks the tang of the sea—"Square and Compass," "Ship's Wheel," "Ocean Wave," "Storm at Sea," "Rolling Star"—these all come from coastwise ancestry. And by the way, the very Ship's Wheel of Cape Cod is called Harvest Sun in Pennsylvania.

The easiest quilts to make are perhaps four-patches upon which so many little girls have learned to sew, and "brick work," that boon plan of piecing for the woman who has a lot of "sample" oblongs all shaped alike. Brick work is simply sewing into shallow rows a strip of equal size oblongs, then jogging the seam half way over for the next row, etc. Four patches are 2 dark and 2 light squares joined checkerboard fashion, and two of these alternated with plain square of equal size to make a large block.

A nine-patch demands that you get four intersections to meet exactly instead of just one as in the four patch. A double nine patch made of tiny squares cut about 1 1-4 inches square makes one of the daintiest quilts imaginable when flowerlike colors are used in profusion with white for the alternate squares. Using all four corners of little pieced ninepatches as well as the center makes it even lovlier.

Quilts like Swastika, Orange Peel, Old Maid's Puzzle, and Windmill are elaborated four patches; while it is easy to trace the nine patch variation in many like Weathervane, Pin Wheels, Maple Leaf, Greek Cross, Jacob's Ladder, etc.

Beggar's Block, Burgoyne's Quilt, and the triangle corners of the Skyrocket are sort of three patch placings. Then come a great group based on the diamond unit, the six and eight pointed stars, the piecing plus applique designs like Honey Bee, Noon Day Lily, Cherry Basket, and Friendship Ring. There are those that take curved seams, Mill Wheel, Rob Peter to Pay Paul, and the French Star and those that demand shallow angle seams like Baby's Blocks and French Bouquet. Double Wedding Ring and Lone Star have the whole quilt top as a unit, although they, too, must work from small pieces to larger.

If you are an applique enthusiast, we have included a few straight "laid on" patterns.

We do hope you will find the very one that appeals to you, and after that another and another as every one has possibilities of real beauty. It's up to you—Choose a pattern!

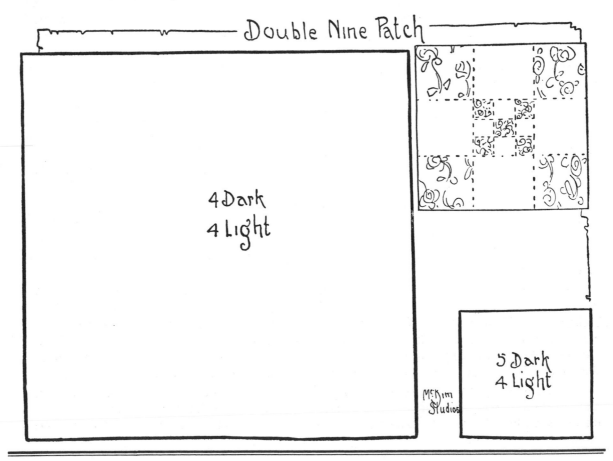

Beggar Block

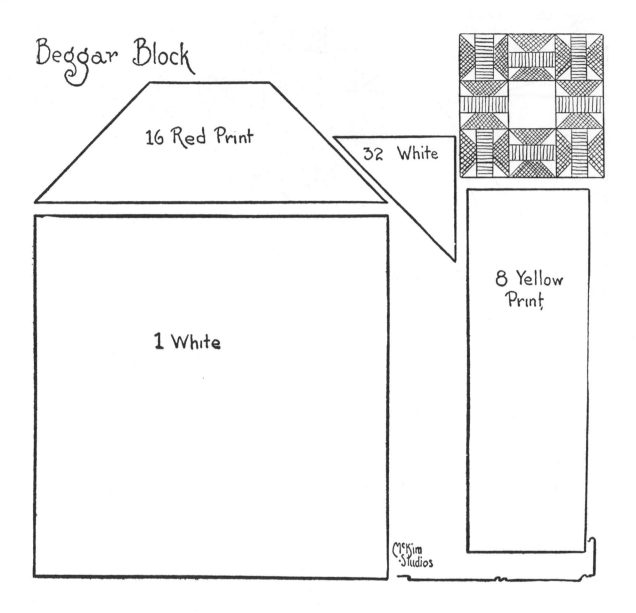

16 Red Print

32 White

8 Yellow Print

1 White

McKim Studios

BEGGAR BLOCK

THIS interesting block harks back to the neighborly custom of begging one's friends for scraps of their frocks, or for the men's old neckties to put into a quilt.

In piecing, first sew the small triangles onto those marked red, to form an oblong exactly the same size as the one marked yellow. Two of these oblongs and one yellow are pieced together as shown to form the small square block. It takes eight of such pieced squares and one plain center to form a beggar's block eleven inches square.

While these are marked in colors for a calico quilt, this is an excellent design to piece with bright colored scraps of silks and wools, set together with black, navy or some dull color in the places marked white. The patterns are the size of the pieces after they have been sewed together, so cut each a seam larger on all sides.

Material Estimate: There are 36 pieced blocks in this quilt set together with white strips 11 by 3¾ inches, plus **seams.** Fill in at the ends of the strips with squares of yellow, add strips top and bottom for length. Your quilt will then complete about 84x91 inches. This will require 1½ yards of yellow, 1 yard red and 6½ yards of white—a total of 9 yards of material.

A narrow Cable or Shell would be right for quilting the strips.

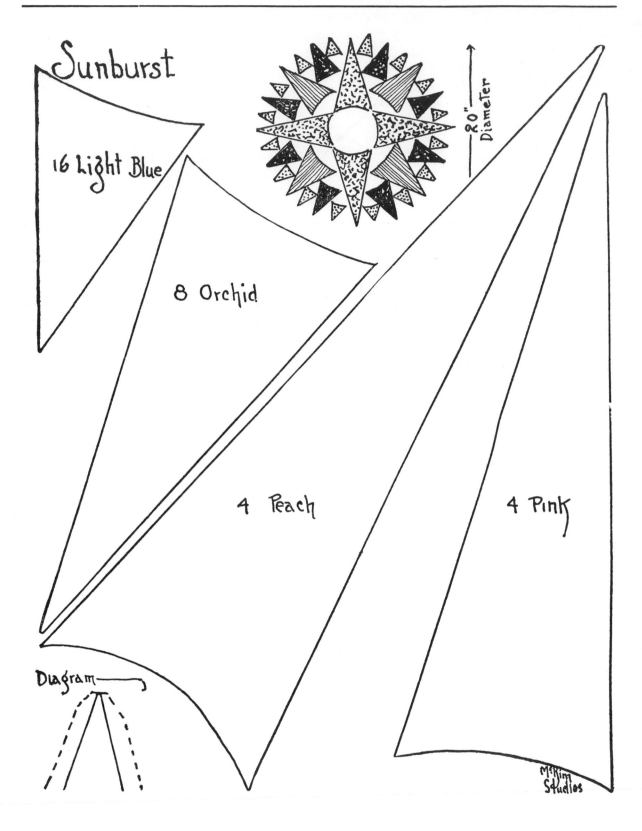

Sunburst

16 Light Blue

8 Orchid

4 Peach

4 Pink

20" Diameter

Diagram

McKim Studios

SUNBURST

A SUNBURST quilt means considerable work to the block, but very few blocks to the quilt. Even as few as four, properly spaced, will make a stunning coverlet, or as many as nine can be used. Half blocks, too, are effective as they look like great rising or setting suns to the edge.

Any gradation of 4 colors which harmonizes with one's room can be used—the yellow and peach tints, greens with blue or yellow or the French—pink-orchid-blue plan as suggested.

The diagram for allowing seams to a sharp angle is helpful as this is a design of acute angles and must be trimmed down accordingly to avoid unwieldy points on the rays.

To place the Sunburst rays on the large background block—22 inches to 36 inches even—crease it in halves and fourths both ways and place the points on creased lines for accuracy.

Material Estimate: By using four 30-inch white squares plus a 9-inch border all around, your quilt will finish about 78 by 78 inches. The border is divided as follows: A 3-inch strip of peach next to quilt center, a 2-inch strip of orchid and then a 4-inch strip of light blue on the outside. This will require 2½ yards of peach, 1-3 yard pink, 1 2-3 yards orchid, 2 yards of light blue and 3½ yards white—a total of 10 yards.

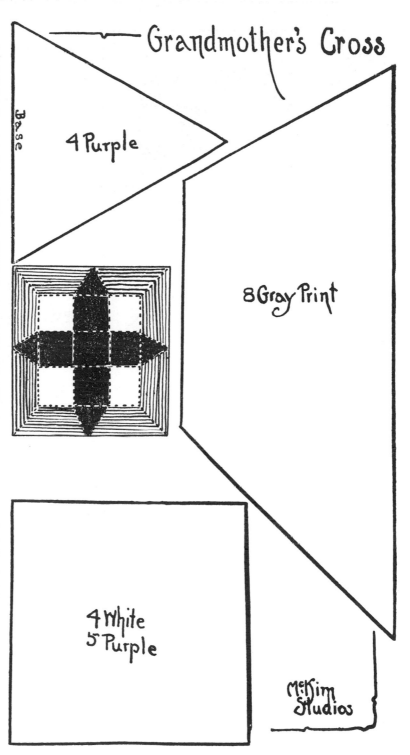

GRANDMOTHER'S CROSS

IT LOOKS like grandmother's idea to to begin with had been a nine-patch with the border inspiration later. This really makes a charming block, 12 inches square completed and is a splendid solution for scraps, "dark, light and medium," for odd woolen pieces to make a heavy "tacked comforter" type of quilt.

Patterns are made of cardboard or blotting paper exactly like the units here given. Mark around these onto material and then cut a seam larger to make the finished block 12 inches square.

The way a quilt sets together may change its whole appearance, for the colors used in the strips and squares bring out those same colors in the quilt block. This quilt would be very nice set together with lavender strips 12 by 2½ inches allowing for seams extra with 2½-inch purple squares filled in at the end of the strips to come at all block intersections.

Material Estimate: Your quilt will have 30 pieced blocks, set together with 44 lavender strips 2½ by 12 inches and 20 purple 2½-inch blocks. There is a 2½-inch lavender border all around. This will require 3½ yards gray print, 1 yard white, 2 yards purple and 2½ yards lavender. This 9 yards includes strips for setting together.

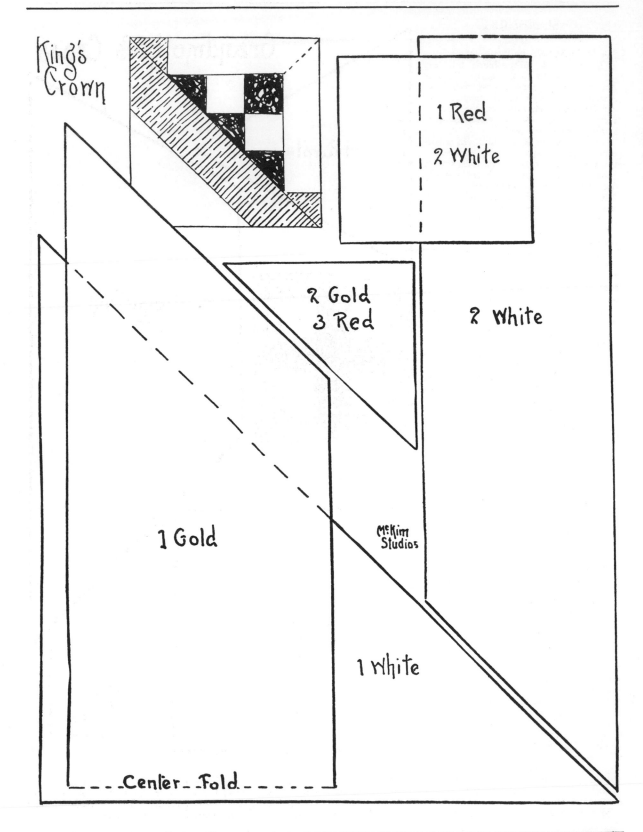

King's Crown

1 Red
2 White

2 Gold
3 Red

2 White

1 Gold

McKim Studios

1 White

Center Fold

KING'S CROWN

NOT really to bedeck the brow of some real king, but to make a quaint old-fashioned coverlet is the purpose of the King's Crown quilt block.

Very simple to piece are these two dissimilar triangles, which, when placed together, make an interesting design square. Grouped for a quilt top they form a more intricate pattern if the position of every other one is reversed, than when set together in the usual checkerboard plan with alternate plain white squares. Size of the King's Crown block is ten inches if seams are allowed in addition to the cutting patterns.

Set together diagonally, with alternate plain white squares, five blocks wide, six blocks long and with a three-inch border all around, this quilt will finish about 76x90 inches. There are 30 pieced blocks, 20 plain blocks, 18 plain half blocks, cut diagonally, and 4 plain fourth blocks for the corners.

Material Estimate: It requires ½ yard red, 1¾ yards gold, and 6½ yards of white to make up this quilt top, or a total of 8¾ yards. A Horn of Plenty or Feather Circle would be interesting on the plain blocks.

WINDMILL AND OUTLINE

OF COURSE this is only the windmill part of the sketched quilt, but so many people have sets of embroidered quilt blocks that we thought this a clever and welcome suggestion for putting them together. Usually just plain blocks are used for this purpose, depending on quilting to add the interest necessary. This windmill is particularly adapted to use in a juvenile quilt as it effects a quaint pattern much like those pin wheel windmills which children love.

A strip is sewed onto a triangle as shown at the bottom of pattern, then 4 triangles make the block, all straight sewing in spite of the staggered effect when finished.

Material Estimate: This pattern does not allow for seams, so they should be added to the sizes given. The block finishes 9½ inches square or 12½ inches on the diagonal. Your quilt requires 42 plain unbleached quilted blocks set together diagonally with 30 whole pieced blocks, 22 half blocks and 4 quarter blocks. If made 6 blocks wide by 7 blocks long, it will finish about 75 by 87 inches. This will require 2½ yards of blue and 5 yards of unbleached, a total of 7½ yards of material.

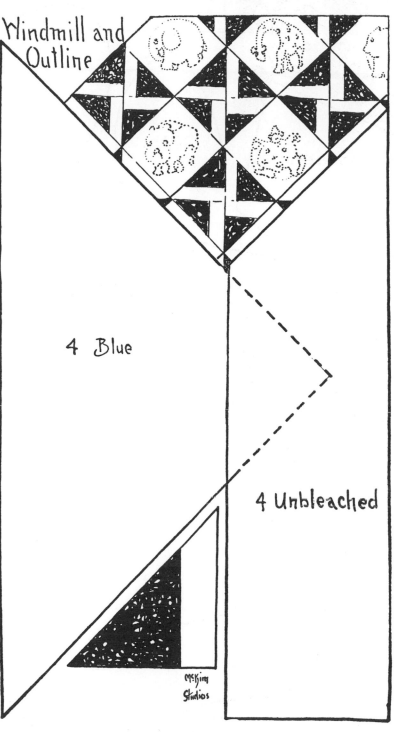

Windmill and Outline

4 Blue

4 Unbleached

McKim Studios

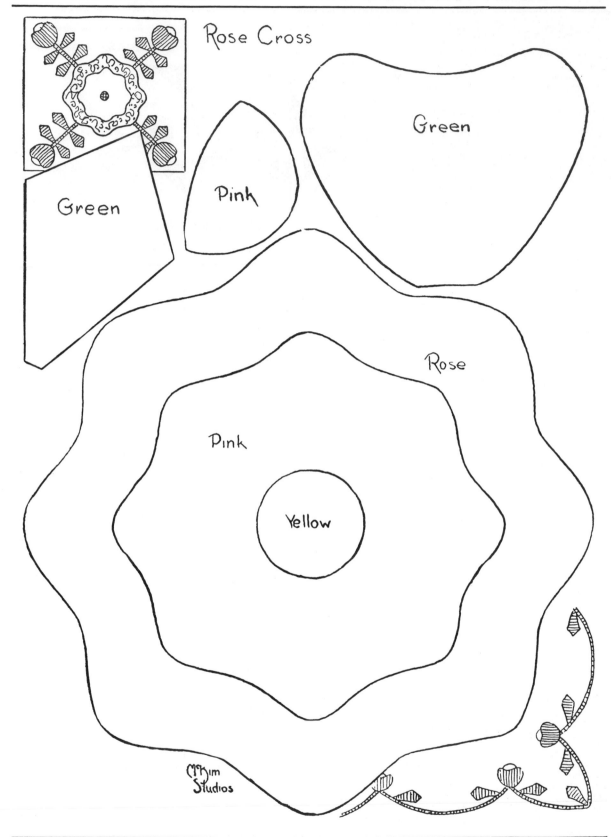

Rose Cross

Green

Pink

Green

Rose

Pink

Yellow

McKim
Studios

ROSE CROSS

APPLIQUE is one of the most popular branches of the quilt making art and it is for lovers of applique that the "Rose Cross" is offered. Unlike piecing, applique offers diversifications and embellishments. The patterns may be made just as elaborate as the maker chooses and her originality has more chance to assert itself.

This pattern shows a decorative combination of a cross motif and a foundation rose pattern. The colors are optional but there is no prettier combination than the ones suggested here in yellow, rose and pink with the leaves

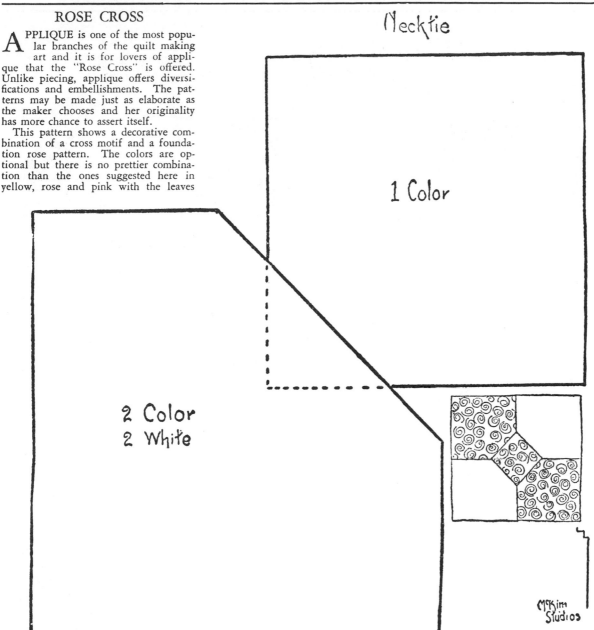

developed in green.

The Rose Cross may be appliqued onto a white 12-inch square and the group of them set together lattice fashion with green strips that are 3 inches wide and 12 inches long when finished, filling in at the end of the strips with a 3-inch rose square. You can also make a 3-inch border all around of the same color, or build an applique one similar to the corner sketch using bias tape for the stem.

Material Estimate: To make the quilt five blocks wide and six blocks long takes 30 blocks. These with the strips make a quilt about 78x96 inches, and will require 4½ yards white, 2½ yards rose, 1 yard pink, 3 of green, and 1-6 yard yellow.

A narrow Cable would be suitable for quilting a 3-inch strip. You can repeat this as many times as is needed for your quilt.

NECKTIE

HERE is the Necktie block for which we have had numerous requests and several patterns supplied. And this block is about as simple to make as a bowknot is to tie.

The idea is to use various scraps of material for the "bows" with a unifying background carrying through in the other two sections of each block. A silk or wool necktie quilt is quite attractive made with dark background or wash goods with white or some continuing tint as yellow print calico, or rose or lavender percale.

Material Estimate: By using 90 pieced blocks set together so the bows all go in the same direction, 9 blocks wide by 10 blocks long, your quilt will finish about 80 by 89 inches. This will require 4 yards of white and 5 yards of color or a total of 9 yards of material. A border may be made by using the small triangles that cut off the corner of the larger block.

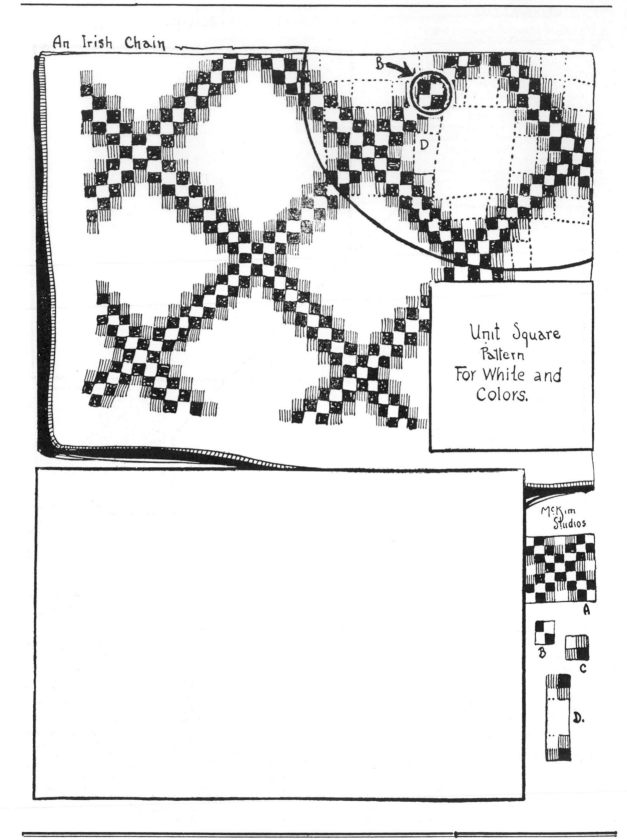

An Irish Chain

Unit Square Pattern For White and Colors.

McKim Studios

A

B

C

D.

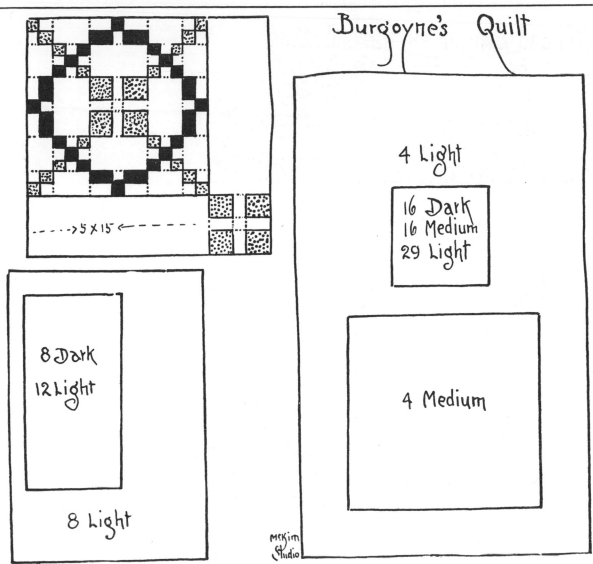

TRIPLE IRISH CHAIN

EVERY enthusiastic quilter has in her collection some sort of Irish Chain. And surely there is a reason, as these do make up into the most effective of old-fashioned counterpanes. There are single, double and even triple varieties—the quilt sketched being the last named.

Any three colors could be used: Wouldn't flame orange and black be modern and gorgeous on apricot tint in sateens? Thirteen pieced blocks A with 12 plain squares about 13 inches square will be enough for a quilt when set together as shown with pieced blocks B and D. C is the pieced ends added to the large oblong pattern to make D. Borders may be added to achieve any desired size.

Cut a seam larger than the patterns here given, as the finished blocks should be at least these sizes.

Material Estimate: Supposing we make the quilt white, with the dark chains red and outer row light green. Allow about 6 yards of white, 2 of red and 1½ of green for a full size quilt top.

A 12-inch Feather Circle can be used on the large open spaces—or the Dove of Peace, or any other design which fits into a square diagonally placed.

BURGOYNE'S QUILT

ALTHOUGH General Burgoyne was a British soldier and not under the American colors at all, the quilt which some way is associated with his name would be really effective in red, navy and white.

A Burgoyne block is composed of a number of smaller units, four patches, nine patches, plains and an odd oblong six patch. Put together according to the plan shown they form a beautiful pattern 15 inches square if seams are added to the cutting units given. Twenty blocks set together with light strips 5 inches wide with a pieced block of medium and light at the corners and bordered with the same makes a quilt top about 85 by 105 which makes a quilt long enough to fold over the pillows to form a spread.

Material Estimate: This quilt takes 20 pieced blocks set together with 49 strips 5 by 15 inches and 30 small pieced 5-inch squares. It will require 1 yard of dark material, 2¼ yards medium and 5 yards of light, a total of 8¼ yards which includes material for setting together.

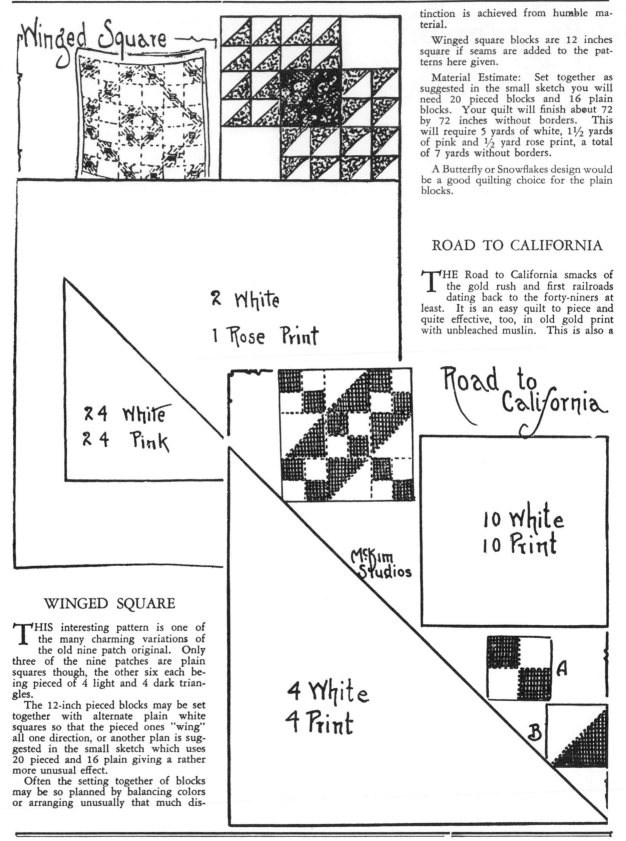

Winged Square

2 White
1 Rose Print

24 White
24 Pink

4 White
4 Print

McKim Studios

Road to California

10 White
10 Print

A

B

tinction is achieved from humble material.

Winged square blocks are 12 inches square if seams are added to the patterns here given.

Material Estimate: Set together as suggested in the small sketch you will need 20 pieced blocks and 16 plain blocks. Your quilt will finish about 72 by 72 inches without borders. This will require 5 yards of white, 1½ yards of pink and ½ yard rose print, a total of 7 yards without borders.

A Butterfly or Snowflakes design would be a good quilting choice for the plain blocks.

ROAD TO CALIFORNIA

THE Road to California smacks of the gold rush and first railroads dating back to the forty-niners at least. It is an easy quilt to piece and quite effective, too, in old gold print with unbleached muslin. This is also a

WINGED SQUARE

THIS interesting pattern is one of the many charming variations of the old nine patch original. Only three of the nine patches are plain squares though, the other six each being pieced of 4 light and 4 dark triangles.

The 12-inch pieced blocks may be set together with alternate plain white squares so that the pieced ones "wing" all one direction, or another plan is suggested in the small sketch which uses 20 pieced and 16 plain giving a rather more unusual effect.

Often the setting together of blocks may be so planned by balancing colors or arranging unusually that much dis-

very good pattern in which to use odd scraps of material, setting them together with alternate plain squares so the dark band with triangle follows diagonally across the quilt one way, and the small dark squares do the same thing in the opposite direction. Surely the Road to California must have had many by-ways leading therefrom!

Each block is 12 inches square, really a nine-patch made of five small blocks A with four B. Cutting patterns are made of cardboard from the ones here given. These do not allow for seams if making a 12-inch block.

Material Estimate: If you make your quilt six blocks wide by seven blocks long it will finish 72x84 inches. By setting together with alternate white blocks you will have 21 pieced blocks and 21 plain. It will require 2½ yards of print and 6 yards of white material.

Snowflakes or a Horn of Plenty would make attractive quilting patterns for the plain blocks.

WHIRLWIND

"WHIRLWIND" and "Pinwheel" often mean the same thing in quilt vernacular, although we'll admit there is considerable difference in real life!

This is a very simple design with small triangles sewing into a larger one which joins with a large print triangle to form a square—one fourth of the finished block. If scrap material is being used, make each block of one print with white or a plaint tint. Keep the prints all about the same light or dark value; variety in hues is charming but some light with some dark blocks makes an ugly quilt.

Cardboard patterns are made matching the triangles here given, and these are used to mark around onto cloth. Then cut a bit larger as these do not allow for seams. The finished blocks are about 8 inches square, and may be set together with strips or plain blocks as desired. However, with plain blocks set diagonally on the quilt, which finishes with half squares of course, is really the approved plan for whirlwind.

Material Estimate: If you set your pieced blocks together with plain white blocks on the diagonal using 7 blocks across and 8 blocks long, your quilt will finish about 78 by 90 inches. It will take 56 pieced blocks, 42 plain whole blocks, 26 plain half blocks (cut on diagonal), and four plain quarter blocks for the corners. This will require 1¾ yards print and 7 yards of white, a total of 8¾ yards. The Cherry Basket perforated pattern No. 327 at 25c would fit the plain blocks for quilting.

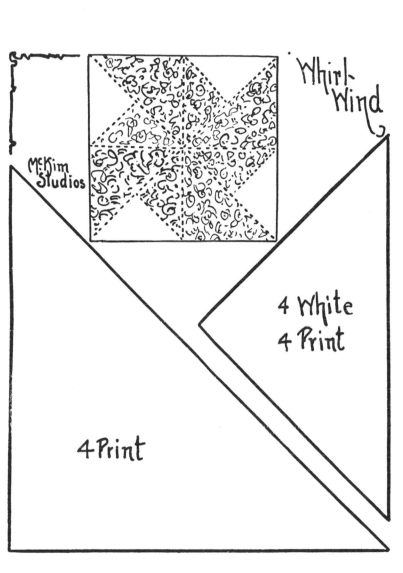

Whirl-Wind

McKim Studios

4 White
4 Print

4 Print

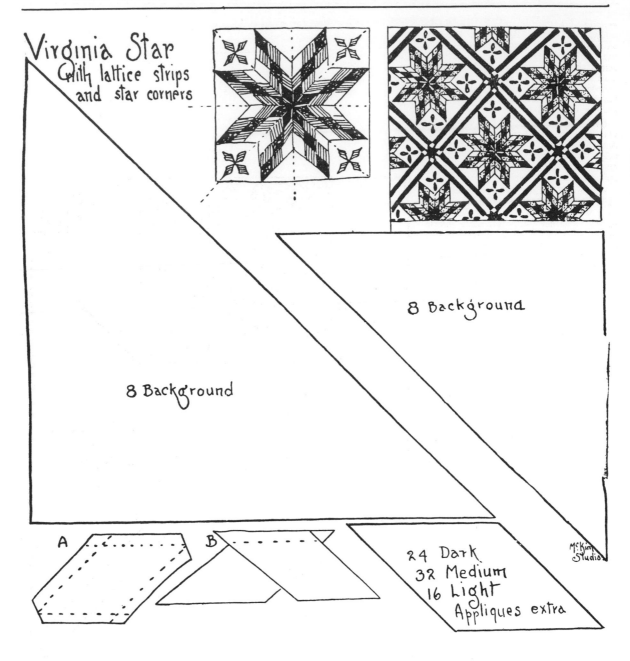

Virginia Star
With lattice strips
and star corners

8 Background

8 Background

A

B

24 Dark
32 Medium
16 Light
Appliques extra

McKim Studio

VIRGINIA STAR

THIS is a really wonderful block, even without the corner appliques or decorative "set" as quilt makers used to call the blocks or strips with which pieced blocks are put together.

The Virginia Star is pieced first by making a large diamond of nine small diamonds, sewed together with edges placed as in sketch B. One of each size background triangle is then added as shown to make a right angle triangle which is half of the square which forms a quarter of the entire block. This is shown by the extended dotted lines of the block. Appliques which are cut from the same unit diamond without adding seams may be added as sketched.

Seams should be added to all other parts and the block will then finish 16 inches square. Lattice strips should finish 1½ inches wide or the strip of three 4½ inches. This makes the small corner stars right to cut from the same unit diamond pattern.

If you set your blocks together diagonally with 4½-inch strips you will have a quilt 3 blocks long and 3 wide finishing about 84 by 84 inches. This will take 13 whole pieced blocks, 8 half blocks and 36 strips each 16 inches long.

Material Estimate: Background white 5 yards, medium 2 yards, (applique material not included) dark 3 yards, and light 1¼ yards, a total of 11¼ yards for the complete quilt.

QUILT MATERIALS

TO BEGIN WITH, I want to say something as trite as it is important and that is, "Use the very best materials that you can afford for any and all handwork." Extravagance is never smart, but good quilt materials are not expensive. It's the sleazy ones, unreliable dyes and starched cloth that prove expensive in the end.

Wash goods is gauged by the number of threads per square inch, "68-72" is a fair grade of percale, "80 square" is excellent, the weight we usually use and some of the very fine imported ginghams run to "120 square."

A firm weave is imperative where one is cutting small triangles and diamonds where part of each block must be bias. Imagine trying to fit bias sides of rayon crepe or voile onto squares and you can see how totally unfitted such scraps are for quilt making. Coarse linens, crash weight cretonne, and pongee unless deeply seamed ravel out too easily to be suitable. Romper cloth and any others that border onto ticking texture are too close weave and heavy to quilt well. Cheap ginghams will shrink enough to pucker in a quilt top. So to the firm weave must be added soft texture. "Buty chine" is a permanent luster satine of finest quality which we recommend for excellent results. The finest materials certainly do make the loveliest quilts.

The dye problem is mastered with a reasonable amount of care as "vat dyes" are usual in even very inexpensive goods. "Commercially fast" the dealer will say, which means with any reasonable care they will not run. Very few manufacturers will absolutely guarantee color, and where they do replace, they have told us it was often a case of sub-standard black thread which had spotted with washing. Quilts are naturally difficult things to launder. A wisp of silk undies may be in, out, and dry in next to no time, but a quilt with cotton filler, top and lining all stitched plumply together goes in for no such speedy procedure. When it gets wet it stays that way long enough to try colors to their limits. We have had quilt colors, yellows and reds "bleed" into the white and in subsequent tubbings clear again to white. For the "priceless" quilts we suggest the French dry-cleaning establishments.

The rather violent coloring of many heirloom quilts is due to their makers' belief that only oil red, oil green and oil yellow were considered reliable enough to use. Sometimes indigo blue was admitted to this favored fast group.

The history of quilt materials is almost as varied and fascinating as the history of quilt names. For instance, our chintz may be traced back through various family connections and changes of name to the "India Chinces" brought over from India by the East India Trading Company. This very fine cotton material was charmingly designed in much the same motifs of Paisley fame. The Persian influence, particularly the "Persian Pear" which women called the "pickle pattern" or "gourds," peacock feather designs, with pineapple, pomegranates and certain exquisitely unreal but lavish flowers all bespeak the Oriental influence. Chintz came both glazed and unglazed.

Imported "unglazed chince" became English made "Flowered Callicoe," and then there came a day when the British sheep and flax farmers framed legislation making it unlawful to produce or wear this cotton stuff so beloved of the feminine heart! This stringent law raised such a storm from the ladies that in due time the ban was modified to a tax, but still unpopular. A few of these taxes on tea, stamps, etc., you will recall bore the fruit of real history on both sides of the Atlantic.

There is a long list of woven cloths advertised from 1715 on, "Demities," "Fustians," "Muslings," "Cambricks," different sorts of "Duck," "Lawn," "Searsucker," "Pealong" the ancestor of longcloth and Nankeen who begat "Blue Denim"! All of these and many more found their way into patchwork but the dearest and most suitable of all was calico. An author who treats this history in full, writes that "the mainstay of the patchworker was from 1700 to 1775 callicoe, from 1775 to 1825 calicoe, and from 1825 to 1875 calico!"

The great majority of quilts are usually made of wash cotton materials, although silks are sometimes used in such patterns as Log Cabin, Grandmother's Fan, or the Friendship Ring, where one's friends are called upon to help furnish beautiful bits to make the patterns as variegated as possible. Woolens, even good parts of worn garments are excellent for the heavy type of coverlet, and such designs as Steps to the Altar, or Grandmother's Cross are suitable. Woolens are so apt to be dull, "practical" colors, that it is imperative to have some certain unit of red, bright green, orange or such in each block.

While cotton broadcloth, percales, or fine gingham, the calico prints and such, are used with muslin for wash quilts, many women maintain that soft satine really makes the most gorgeous quilt of all. When the time comes to quilt you will know why we stress soft materials and why lustrous satine which catches light on every little silk-like puff between quilting designs is so beloved.

INTERLINING MATERIAL

The warmth of the quilt will depend upon the thickness and kind of interlining you use. If warmth is desired, have a thick interlining which means that the quilting lines must be farther apart. If the quilting is to be close and elaborate the interlining must be thin. When a bed cover of exceptional warmth is needed, use a comfort bat of cotton or wool. This will be too thick to push the needle through easily, making even stitches impossible. Instead of quilting, this coverlet must be tacked or tufted.

Cotton batting is most commonly used as interlining for quilts. One bat is enough for a quilt, unless it is over size. Four bats will make three extra sized quilts by using the length for width and piecing out the length. Sometimes a lightweight cotton blanket or flannelette is used, but the quilt will not have that soft puffiness that cotton gives. The best bat costs a trifle more but the finished quilt is a thing of beauty. If flannelette is used for padding, the breadths of cloth should be whipped together, as a seam will cause an ugly lump in the quilt. We never use sheet wadding as a filler for a cover that is to be quilted; it is much too stiff for easy work.

LINING AND THREAD

As to the lining or backing, colors are quite popular, lemon yellow, baby blue, or whatever tint harmonizes with the quilt top. White or unbleached were always used on the old-time quilts. But white or tinted, the lining must be soft, unstarched either wide sheeting or strips of 36-inch width inconspicuously seamed, to use with wash material tops. Satine is best with satine, while a silk quilt may be lined with wool challis, with a silk that will not cut out, or even with dark cotton chintz where a blanket interlining is used.

Thread is the only other "material"; this is usually No. 50 white for piecing, finer or in matching mercerized tints for applique. For machine piecing use finer thread, perhaps 70. Numbers 50 or 60 are the standard quilting threads, white in almost all cases, although quilting on fine satine is lovely in No. 70. A No. 50 crochet twist in colors is effective for quilting on silk or rayon comforts.

Workmanship should be, like materials, the "best you can afford." This may mean machine stitching for busy women, or the finest of handwork which we prize so highly in heirloom quilts. Close stitches are imperative in quilt making. We certainly want no ripped corners where cotton will pop out, or pulled seams in our quilt top.

CUTTING AND PIECING
CUTTING

AFTER the pattern and material are decided, the problem of cutting out our quilt is next. This is conceded to be the least interesting and most tedious part of quilt making; however, it is certainly not a step that can be hurried as blocks must be cut exact. There is no alternative to this. The very week I am writing this there came a gingham diamond clear from Montana to me in Missouri, from a woman asking, "What's wrong with this pattern I got from a friend—it won't make a blazing star"! And indeed it would not; the angle was too acute. Eight of them would sew together like a saucer, and no two sides of the diamonds were alike in length, the shortest varying from the longest by 5-8 inch!

In the patterns here given the angles and curves have been determined. Lengths are fairly accurate, although seam allowances may vary, and it does make a difference where a certain piece is due to fit. Two triangles, equal sides together should be cut equal, but a triangle against a square of equal length will finish a seam narrow at each end unless extra allowance is made on the triangle.

We suggest that you lay tissue paper over the cutting pattern in the book, allow seams if you want the block to finish the size given, then make up one test block. You may have to change the relation of pattern sides in some cases before transferring your proven patterns onto the cardboards which will be traced around for marking out all parts. It is a matter of preference again whether your master cardboards be the cutting or sewing size. Some like to cut on the pencil line and gauge their seams back from this. Others prefer to cut a seam out from lines which are penciled onto the wrong side of the cloth, then sew back on these lines assuring exact finished sizes. Blotting paper makes excellent patterns for marking around on any cloth that slips easily, as it clings. Keep all angles sharp: Many an old-time pattern has gradually changed in character and name by being marked around until the points wore down into curves, or shallow curves into deeper ones.

True bias and edges cut with the weave are imperative for right triangle sides, and on equi-angular triangles one side must be with the weave. Squares and oblongs must be with the weave of course. In all of our ready cut quilts this is accurately followed. The center threads in the rays of the "Rising Sun" run directly from center base to apex.

After one sample block is correctly made it is often advantageous to cut or tear the quilt borders from yardage before cutting new material into block units. You know about the area of cloth one given block takes and can easily estimate enough of each color for the number of blocks required. Hence, border strips may be torn to require less piecing before cutting the blocks.

About one yard is required for binding a plain quilt, this cuts on the true bias into strips about 1½ inches wide. Corners are left from this which also may be cut into block units. Allow 1½ yards for binding scallop edge quilts.

Cloth should be smooth to cut, so iron any wrinkled material before laying on the patterns. Hold the cardboard firmly in place, mark around evenly with pencil on light goods or with French chalk on dark colors. Draw a thread to straighten cloth when necessary, and cut very carefully. Inaccuracies in cutting are as fatal in their way in this operation as in the so-called "major operations"! And "lastly" cut economically; a thrifty cutter has mighty few scraps left after her patterns have been laid on to the best advantage.

THE APPLIQUE PROCESS

IN CUTTING applique parts the only special admonition is to clip in well to the folding back line on any concave curve—to keep stem widths even and mark accurately, of course. Bias tape is often substituted for cut stems. The sewing part of the applique work is most important. Some like an exact unit of cardboard to press edges back over with a hot iron. A creased edge that bastes back as you go is fairly simple to do. For circles or other convex edges it is best to run a fine gathering thread very near the edge and full it back to an even fold. This is perfect for creasing back circles like the center in the ready cut "Rising Sun."

All applique quilts baste first, building up the design, tucking leaf ends under stems, covering stem ends with buds or flowers, and of course these ends which are tucked under do not have to be turned back as the raw edge is covered. The charm of perfect applique is to keep it free from puckers.

When a block or section of the design is basted into place, whip around the edge with tiny blind stitches using thread which matches the material if possible. Fancy stitching such as blanket-stitch, chain or buttonhole is seldom advised. If you want your quilt to have the effect of the old-time "laid on" variety, choose the inconspicuous way of fine workmanship and no embroidery. Applique for other purposes, on aprons, decorative linens and such is usually more effective when buttonholed around, and of course it is a matter of taste in the quilt problem. There is no *one* way to combine colors, to piece or to quilt, and your idea may be as right as another.

PIECING

Piecing a quilt top is not such a formidable task. Really a knowledge of plain sewing, accuracy and neatness are all that are required to add to that desire to make it yourself. What little helpful tricks and methods we have learned we pass on to you. The special instructions given with each pattern tell you how to build that particular block, unless it is an obviously simple plan.

The two pieces to be sewed together must be accurately placed and firmly held. Triangle or diamond points extend out exactly the width of a seam, as you will find by sewing them. Seams absolutely must be even. If you like a quarter inch seam, and start that way, keep all of them so. Three-sixteenths is the perfect width for ordinary materials in my opinion, and this width is easily gauged by a sewing machine foot. Some makers of exquisite quilts use 1-8 inch strong for their seams, and when the material is very close weave this width will hold. The less material to bunch up underneath at quilting time, the smoother the finished quilt will be. A knot or back stitch may be used to start each little piecing seam, and each must be well fastened at the end, as that seam end will be part of another seam later.

Two bias edges together will stretch unless your sewing thread fulls them a trifle taut. It is better to sew a weave thread against a bias edge when possible as in joining diamonds for the eight pointed star designs. Even a thirty-secondth of an inch if added to several diamonds on one side of a big Lone Star diamond, and the same number less several times on an adjacent point, will throw the plan awry. Seams must be even. Quilt piecing is a most precise craft where a few tiny inaccuracies add quickly into a total of ugly stretch or puckers.

Pieced sections should be pressed; the seam turned to one side is easier and we think better than trying to open all seams flat. Protruding angles may be trimmed as you piece, which will also add to the smoothness of your top.

Your decision as to a seam width and whether or not you allow seams extra to the unit patterns here given will change the estimated sizes a bit. But there is no one size a finished quilt must be. If your block finishes 13 inches, where we say about 12, that will simply mean that 36-inch material will not cut the alternate blocks to so good an advantage, but otherwise your size is just as right as ours.

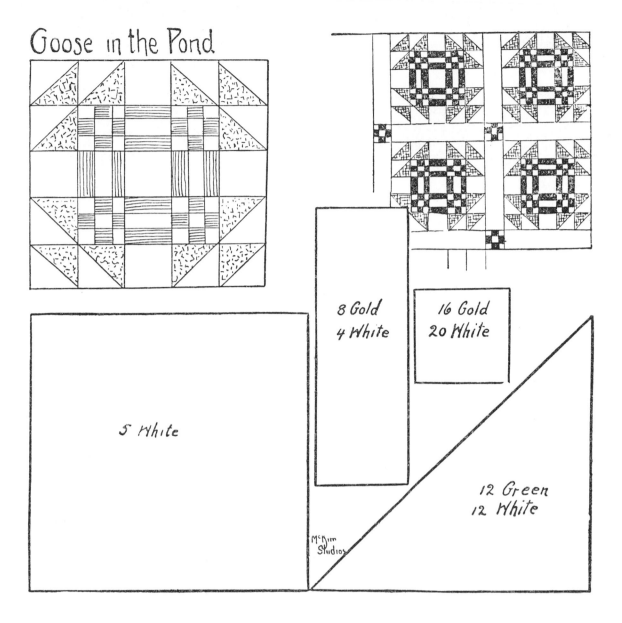

Goose in the Pond

8 Gold
4 White

16 Gold
20 White

5 White

12 Green
12 White

McKim Studios

GOOSE IN THE POND

GOOSE in the Pond is one of those homey old-fashioned names which grace so many patchworks. Historical, geographical, botanical, comical, —names that sparkle with a glint of imagination all of which adds much to the charm of calico cuttings and fine seams. "Lincoln's Platform," "Kansas Troubles," and "Steps to the Altar" sound real enough, but who would know what the nature would be of "Widower's Choice," or "Old Maid's Combination"?

Goose in the Pond is really composed of 25 three-inch squares, 5 of them plain, 12 made of 2 triangles, 4 tiny ninepatches and 3 three-layer strip squares. This makes a block 15 inches square, as shown in the sketch below the name. Set together with white strips 3 inches wide and tiny ninepatches at the corners it takes about 16 blocks with borders added for a quilt.

Colors may be chosen to fit into any scheme, but sizes should be kept small for this pattern. Cut the cloth just a seam larger than the four patterns here given as these are to be finished sizes. This is a good selection for a patchwork pillow or tie-on chair seats.

Material Estimate: The quilt includes 16 pieced blocks, each 15 inches square, set together with 24 strips, 15 by 3 inches, with 9 three-inch pieced blocks at the intersections to make the quilt center. This, with a 3-inch border at sides and a 6-inch border at the ends, will finish about 75 by 81 inches. You will need 1½ yards of green material, 2½ yards of gold, and 6 yards of white, which includes the border and strips.

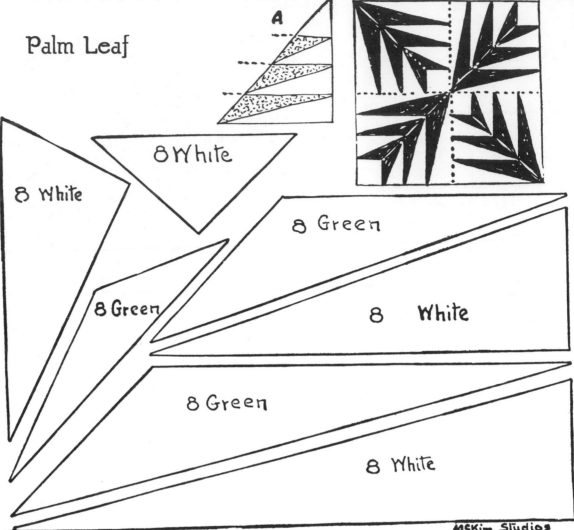

Palm Leaf

A

8 White

8 White

8 Green

8 Green

8 White

8 Green

8 White

McKim Studios

PALM LEAF

SOMETHING entirely different again in the field of patchwork is this gorgeous block, the palm leaf. This pattern is sometimes called "Hosannah" which ties it more closely to the religious significance which prevails in so many of the old-time quilt names.

A quilt top made entirely of pieced blocks would be exquisite. Twenty-five 12-inch blocks set diagonally would finish with 18 half blocks (large triangles) and four quarter blocks into a quilt top about 68 inches square. A 5-inch white border with a 2-inch green border outside of that would make it about 82 inches square complete.

Each block is pieced first in a triangle like sketch A, then two of these to form a square, which is one-fourth of an entire block. If the colored material be a print with right and wrong sides, half of the dark patterns will have to be marked reverse.

Material Estimate: Four and one-half yards of green and six yards of white will cut this quilt, borders and all. Total, 10½ yards.

Quilting follows the line of the seams, about ¼ inch each side of each one all around and makes a pattern of slender triangles very effective even on the reverse side.

THE STRING QUILT

THIS is a very interesting quilt, suitable for using long, narrow scraps, such as old silk neckties or wash materials left along selvedges and such.

The kite-shaped center blocks should be all alike in color, and if the strips repeated the same five hues each time it would make a lovely pattern. When using odd scraps they should be kept dark, medium and light as suggested. This quilt is made of all pieced blocks or blocks set together with 1¼-inch strips. In either case there is a pronounced pattern where four blocks join

which makes an unusually lovely repeat.

The pattern appears to be complex, whereas it is really not difficult but just a bit tedious and exacting. The five graduated pieces sew together in order to form an isosceles triangle. Two of these join onto the long sides of a kite-shaped piece to form a right triangle, which is one fourth of the block. Seams must be added to the cutting patterns here given.

Each String block finishes about 15 inches square; therefore, thirty pieced blocks set together, 5 blocks wide by 6 blocks long, and the quilt will finish about 75 by 90 inches, or considerably less may be used with a border.

Material Estimate: A String Quilt would be lovely with a peach tint background, deep coral for the dark, and apple green for the medium and ivory for light. Allow 3 yards of background color, 1½ yards of light, 2 yards of dark, and 2 yards of medium, 8½ yards total.

The String Quilt

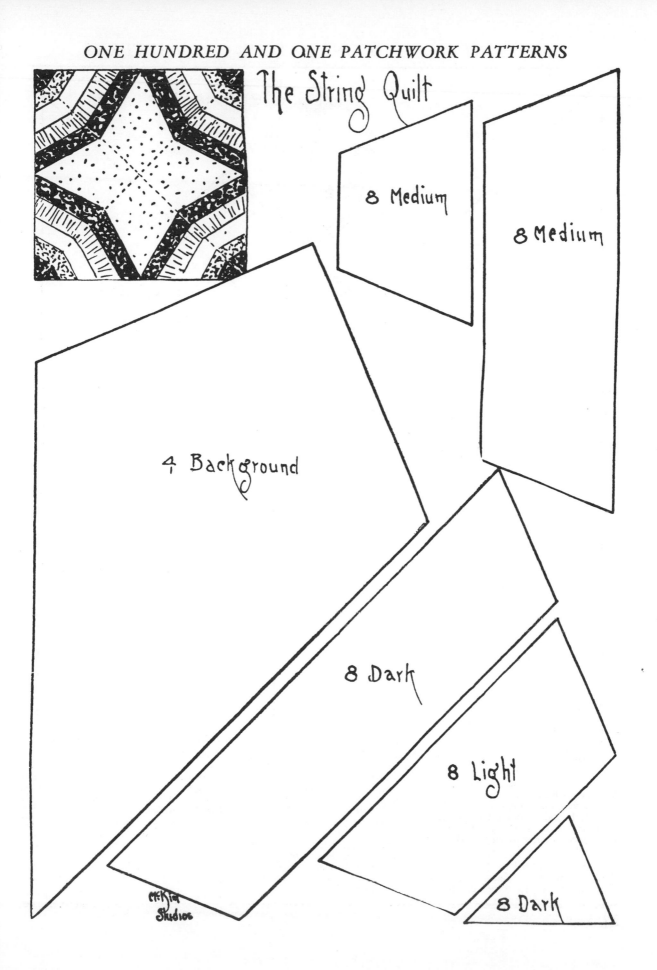

8 Medium

8 Medium

4 Background

8 Dark

8 Light

8 Dark

McKim
Studios

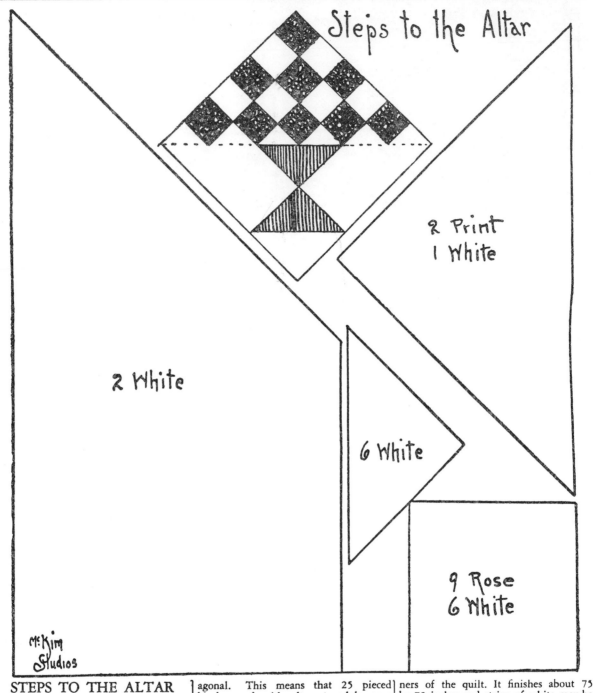

Steps to the Altar

2 Print
1 White

2 White

6 White

9 Rose
6 White

McKim
Studios

STEPS TO THE ALTAR

OF ALL the quaint and cheerful names bestowed upon the old-time patchwork, "Steps to the Altar" is certainly about the most romantically cheering! It is all straight line seaming too, and a very charming block when done.

If seams are added to the pattern as given, each block will finish about 10½ inches square, or 15 inches on the di-agonal. This means that 25 pieced blocks used with alternate plain ones will make a quilt top. The alternate plain ones are much enhanced by fancy quilting while pieced blocks may be done in straight lines following the seams of the pieced squares and triangles.

Material Estimate: The quilt contains 25 pieced blocks set together diagonally with 16 plain 10½-inch blocks, 16 plain half blocks, cut diagonally, and 4 plain quarter blocks for the four corners of the quilt. It finishes about 75 by 75 inches and strips of white may be added at top and bottom for additional length. You will require ½ yard of print, 1 1-3 yards rose and 5 2-3 yards white material. Total 7½ yards.

A Feather Circle would be lovely on the alternate blocks, and so would any design which adapts to diagonal blocks.

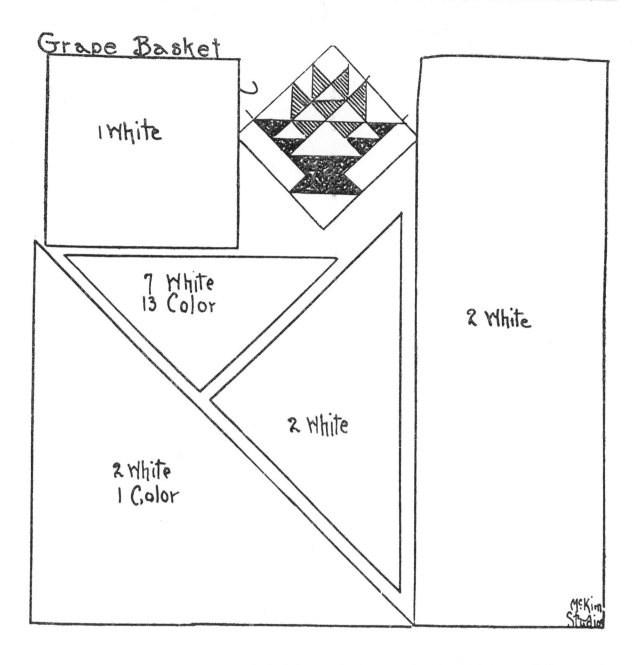

GRAPE BASKET

BASKET quilts are always popular. There are several charming versions easy to piece. The main part of this one is a 4-patch of pieced squares as indicated by the extended lines. To this the long strips with a small triangle on the ends are added,

then the final bottom triangle to complete.

The grape basket finishes into a block ten inches square if seams are added to the unit patterns here given.

It should be set together on the diagonal with alternate plain squares and half squares of white to the edges. Twenty-five pieced blocks plus a 6-inch border and binding makes a full-sized quilt.

Material Estimate: If using green for the basket and 4 dark triangles, with lavender for the lighter color triangles, allow 2 yards of green and 1 1-3 yards of lavender. Six yards of white will make a border, the plain blocks and pieced ones, too. Total 9 1-3 yards.

An eight-inch Feather Circle would be attractive on the plain blocks, with a Peacock Fan on the border.

Ribbon Border Block

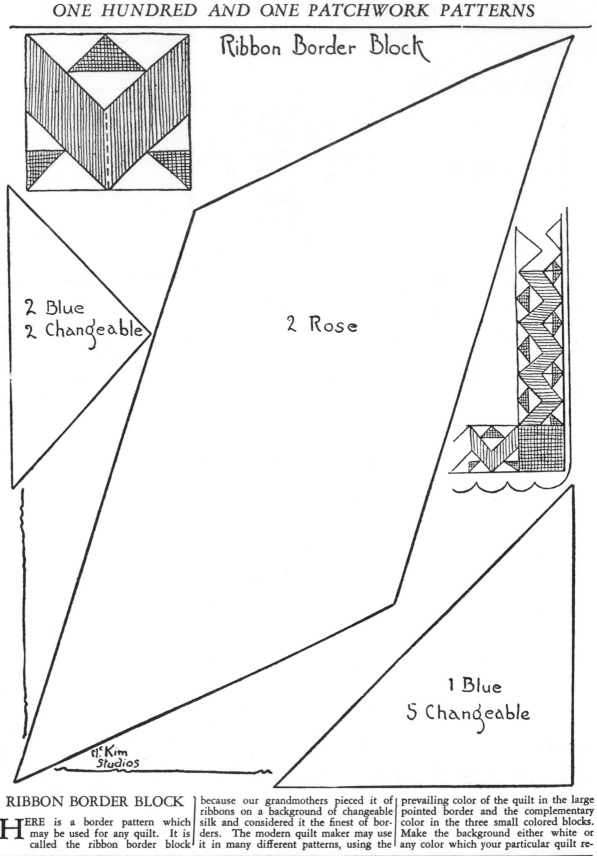

2 Blue
2 Changeable

2 Rose

1 Blue
5 Changeable

McKim
Studios

RIBBON BORDER BLOCK

HERE is a border pattern which may be used for any quilt. It is called the ribbon border block because our grandmothers pieced it of ribbons on a background of changeable silk and considered it the finest of borders. The modern quilt maker may use it in many different patterns, using the prevailing color of the quilt in the large pointed border and the complementary color in the three small colored blocks. Make the background either white or any color which your particular quilt re-

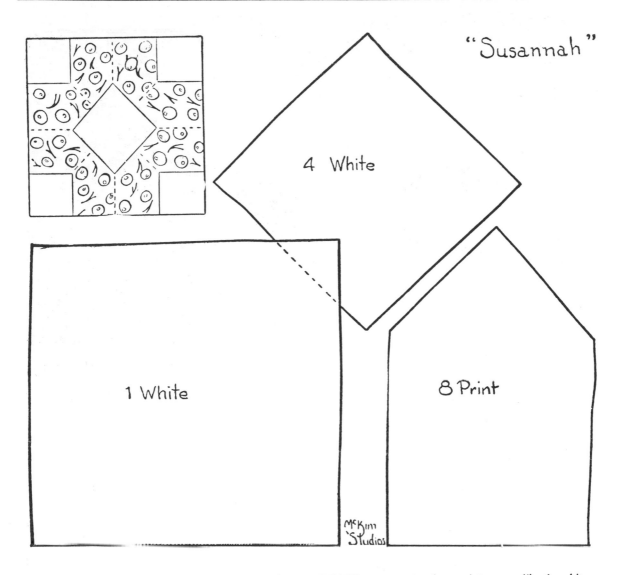

"Susannah"

4 White

1 White

8 Print

McKim Studios

SUSANNAH

DATING back to the days when our pioneer fathers and mothers were crossing the plains in wagon trains, we have Susannah, the rollicking song, and Susannah, the quilt block Perhaps the peaked print blocks were from the silhouettes of formidable mountain peaks ahead with stretches of plain before their angular summits. And altogether the Susannah block forms a cross. Don't think those brave imaginative quilt makers would overlook that symbolism, or the tortuous paths that the white squares form when it is all set together with plain white blocks!

This is not an easy block to piece, cut as it is shown, copied from an old pattern. It seems that it would be easier to have print squares like the white ones, and double-sized triangles added to the center square. But that would be decapitating the mountains and modernizing the prairie trail, and the quilt's owner said hesitatingly, "No, we did it this other way!"

A Susannah block finishes 10½ inches square if seams are added to the above sizes. Seven blocks by eight, or eight wide by nine long may be used for the quilt top, alternating plain and pieced squares.

Material Estimate: Six yards of white with 2½ yards of print is ample for a large sized quilt in this design.

A Tulip or any other flower would be interesting on the plain squares if an easy, rather open pattern is desired.

quires. You may find this 9-inch border useful in making a modernistic looking striped quilt. Piece several long strips of border design and set them together with plain strips the same width and length.

Although this is an old-fashioned pattern, the suggested colors and materials are for a most modern coverlet, the couch robe or even the down puff for a chaise lounge. A center width of quilted taffeta in changing tones in blue and rose, combined with silk in plain blue and plain rose for the border blocks would make a most delightful summer throw or afghan. Made of 36-inch silk it would finish 54 inches wide. Either a plain binding or scallops could finish the edge.

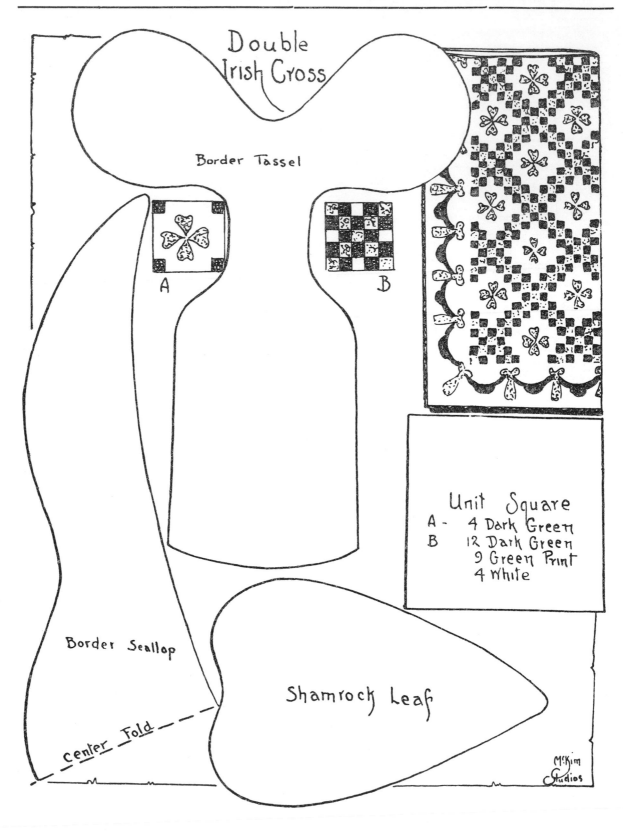

Double Irish Cross

Border Tassel

A

B

Border Scallop

Center Fold

Shamrock Leaf

Unit Square
A - 4 Dark Green
B - 12 Dark Green
9 Green Print
4 White

McKim Studios

DOUBLE IRISH CROSS

THIS is really just a glorified double Irish Chain with the shamrock forming an applique on each of the odd blocks. Then there is the tassel draped scallop border which adds much of elegance to any favorite patchwork. Scallop borders are assured of much better corners than they sometimes get if a pattern is cut in the exact size of one, two or three finished blocks. In this quilt the blocks finish 10 inches square if seams are added to the unit pattern, and the scallop is 10 inches long.

The body of the quilt is self-explantory, a simple alternation of blocks A and B and the coveted "Double Irish" is achieved! Dark green unit squares are appliqued onto the corners of 10-inch white blocks in A while B must be pieced in the exact order shown in the small sketch.

Material Estimate: The quilt includes 24 blocks of A and 25 blocks of B, and finishes about 70 inches square. Add a border from 7 to 10 inches wide, to bring this up to the size you desire. Allow 5 yards of white, 3 yards of dark green and 3 yards of green print.

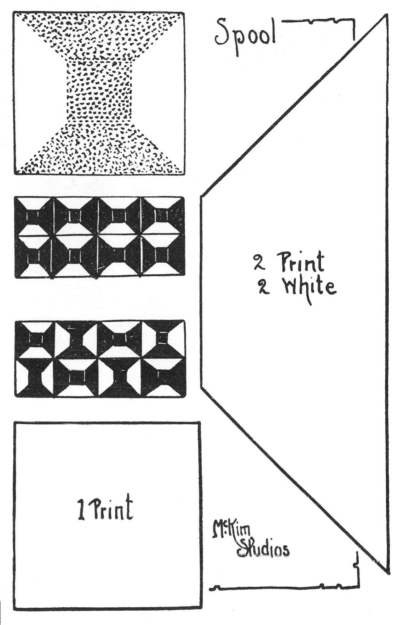

SPOOL

IN THE days of our grandmothers, the spool motif played an important part in the making of wooden beds, stool legs and whatnots. It even was inspiration for the making of this quaint quilt pattern. Imagine how charming a spool coverlet would look on a Jenny Lind or an old-fashioned "spool bed." However, one does not have to possess a bed of either type to make a spool quilt.

These blocks are rather difficult to piece, as the ends of the four-side pieces set into an angle when sewed onto the center block. This could be overcome by changing the pattern so that the center square cuts into 4 triangles, plus seams. By sewing these onto the short sides of the outside pieces, 4 large triangles are formed. These 4 large triangles sewed together to form the 6-inch block make straight sewing all the way. To piece from the pattern as given, sew the short sides of the outside blocks onto the center square, then fold and sew corner seams.

The small diagrams show two methods of setting the finished blocks together. Either method could be used for an all-over pattern of solid blocks or joined into strips 2 blocks wide, the desired length of the quilt and set together with white strips 6 inches wide, to run the length of the bed.

Since we so strongly advocate borders on quilts, why not appropriate a row of spools, like one half of the upper placing for a spool border to use on most any patchwork you happen to be making?

Material Estimate: Allow extra for seams if the blocks are to finish six inches square. Set together 14 blocks wide by 15 blocks long, without plain strips or blocks, it will require 210 pieced blocks and will finish about 84 by 90 inches. You will need 4½ yards of print and 3½ yards of white material. However, you will have a more effective quilt and less work if an all-over center is planned, then a wide band of plain white for fancy quilting, then a spool border and a final row the darker color.

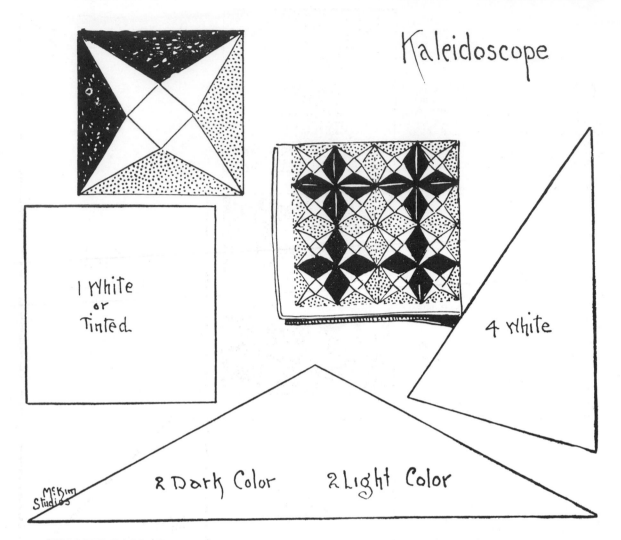

Kaleidoscope

1 White or Tinted

4 White

2 Dark Color   2 Light Color

McKim Studios

KALEIDOSCOPE

AS A CHILD you may have peered into the revolving mystery of a kaleidoscope, where mirrors repeated into alluring prismic forms the wonders of a few bright chips and pebbles. The "kaleidoscope" quilt gives that same bewildering effect and yet it is simple as can be to piece. Of course, it is lots of work, as every block is a pieced one; but these are all exactly alike, six inches square and each four set together as shown to make a block twelve inches square, which is really the unit. This is sometimes called "Amethyst Quilt," when developed in purple, lavender and white.

One cheering thought to the woman who pieces this quilt—she will have a beautiful coverlet without fancy quilting, such as is necessary to enrich a quilt with large, plain squares.

Material Estimate: The quilt contains 168 six-inch blocks, set together 12 blocks wide and 14 blocks long, making a quilt about 72 by 84 inches. You will need 2½ yards of light material, 2½ yards of dark and 4½ yards of white, a total of 9½ yards.

ENGLISH FLOWER GARDEN

A QUILT which is as picturesquely English as Anne Hathaway's cottage is this quaint Flower Garden Applique. It may be made of all variegated flowers in gay prints with yellow centers; or a color plan of coral, turquoise, and gold flowers with green leaves and centers would be lovely. The pot is of green and white check gingham with 16-inch square background blocks of white, or light yellow.

Twenty blocks set together with 3-inch strips of green check in lattice effect make a center about 73 by 89 inches. A 5-inch border all around this brings it to generous size, both to cover pillows and tuck in at the foot. Seams are not allowed.

Material Estimate: You would need 3½ yards of check material, 1-3 yard each of 3 prints or flower tints, 1 yard of green for the leaves and stems and 4 yards of white, a total of 9½ yards.

Quilting would follow the lines of the appliqued design, with perhaps a Shell rounding into each block corner and a narrow Cable quilted along the lattice strips.

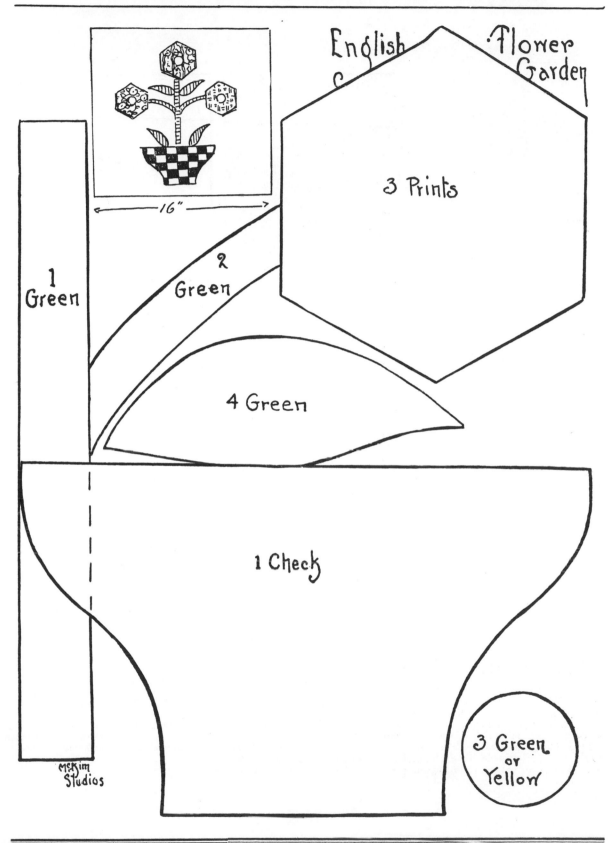

English Flower Garden

3 Prints

16"

1
Green

2
Green

4 Green

1 Check

McKim
Studios

3 Green
or
Yellow

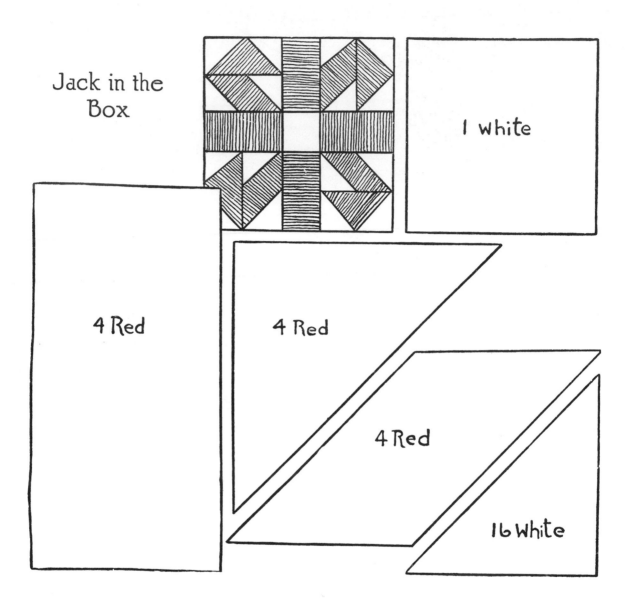

Jack in the
Box

1 white

4 Red

4 Red

4 Red

16 White

JACK IN THE BOX

JACK in the Box is a crisp angular pattern almost as perky as its surprising name. The sketched block shows how easy it is to piece first two white triangles onto a diamond to make a little oblong, then two white triangles added to a red triangle make another, and these two oblongs join together making one corner square. Seams are not allowed so should be added to the sizes given if your blocks are to finish 10 inches square.

Material Estimate: This quilt sets together with alternate plain white ten-inch blocks. We suggest 7 blocks wide by 8 blocks long. A 3-inch border all around will bring the size to about 76 by 86 inches for the complete top. Twenty-eight pieced blocks and twenty-eight plain are used for this plan, requiring 2½ yards of red and 6½ yards of white, which will allow for the border.

A Pineapple or Four Flowers would fit nicely onto the alternate plain 10-inch squares with the pieced blocks quilted to follow the seams.

SETTING TOGETHER

"SETTING TOGETHER" may give a wrong impression to you of romantic mind. Now, as John Fox explains "whar you says 'making a call on a young lady' we says "settin' up with a gal"—an, stranger, we does it!" Well, setting together a quilt means business, too, because the next and final stage is quilting.

The blocks in this book finish all the way from 5 to 20 inches square. Some may be made up according to choice, others must go a definite way to make the quilt top. In quilt parlance "set," the noun, means material and plan other than the pieced blocks. "Set," the verb, means putting together the finished blocks with the "set" (noun). Nowadays, we say "lattice strips" or "alternate squares"; these are the two principal "sets."

The manner of setting together our finished blocks has as much to do with the appearance of the finished quilt as clothes do with the man! Or the old debate question of birth versus environment is paralleled—my blocks are so—what quality will their surroundings bring forth? Take blocks like the "Honey Bee" or "Order Number Eleven," or even a simple "Churn Dash." Visualize them as an all-over, or set slightly apart by inconspicuous white strips, or widened further still by alternate blocks. See how very different these effects are—and how changed again when the dividing strips are dark or pieced into a pattern. So even though you start with an ordinary pattern your quilt may be truly individual when finished.

Some blocks must join edge to edge for an all-over effect as "Beautiful Star" and "Lafayette Orange Peel." Some join but reverse color as "Mill Wheel" and "Rob Peter to Pay Paul." Yet others join all edges of pieced blocks together but change position or placing into a more complex appearing all-over like the "Drunkard's Path" or "Milky Way." A block must have strong individuality to use as a lone repeat this way; such blocks as Dutchman's Puzzle, Goose Tracks, or most any of the basic four patch or nine patch blocks would lose their identity as blocks unless separated by strips or squares of plain. Pieced or applique blocks which alternate with plain squares, usually white, of the same size is the most popular method of setting together. This makes the pattern of each stand out boldly, the design blocks forming a checkerboard pattern with the plain. This is sometimes achieved with block edges parallel to the quilt borders, and must be so in such designs as "House on the Hill" where the block has a top and base definitely so placed. Other patterns have a decided top and bottom on the angle, as the trees, baskets and noon day lily. These are best set together diagonally with alternate squares, finishing with half squares, triangles, at the sides. The quilt called "Monkey Wrench" or "Snail's Trail" does something different again, alternating one whole row with white and the next with colored plain squares, and achieving a most unusual effect thereby. An applique block may alternate with a pieced, as in double Irish Cross.

Strips between, some localities call it "sash work" and others lattice, is the next most popular set. Either three or four inches tear to no waste from 36-inch material and make nice spacing apart for such blocks are French Star, Swastika, Bear's Paw, and dozens of others. When matching the block's background, these space the designs apart inconspicuously. If you want each block to be particularly prominent in itself use a contrasting color or a three-stripe lattice strip as 2½-inch light center with 1¼-inch of dark either side. This is showy for elaborate blocks like the Rising Sun or Skyrocket. The corner joins have to be planned carefully in such a set. Each such square may be plain, a nine patch or even a little pieced star as shown with "Virginia Star," which is very elaborate.

Again the lattice strips may be pieced; diagonally placed squares which fill in with triangles to make a band are effective with such patterns as the "Album" or Bird's Nest where the same band design cuts through that block's center.

Aside from the standard squares and strips, a few quilts must have specially shaped blocks to complete them. Such are the "Rolling Star," "Seven Stars," and "Double Wedding Ring." Our original design number 554 a pieced tulip is in a sort of diamond paned window effect using alternate six sided blocks of white with yellow triangles fitting together into adjoining squares, the whole outlined in black to accent the unusual plan.

A "crazy patch" is made of silks if it be pretentious at all, or from wash scraps for economy of time and cloth. Even this may be made in blocks, but the time honored method was to build on and on until your quilt became a discouraging lap full. A quilt like "Baby's Blocks" is an "allover set" and "Grandmother's Flower Garden," really is too, as it is made entirely of the small hexagons.

The seam which joins blocks in the set is usually the same sort that joins pieces in a block. Right sides of even length are faced together, machine stitched or hand sewed with small, firm stitches, and the seam pressed flat when finished. Sometimes fancy stitching marks the outline of blocks, and you may have seen a "corded quilt" where the block seams finished with a cord run piping. Silk crazy quilts often had all the little blocks embellished with fancy stitching around their irregular shaped edges.

QUILT SIZES

The plan of setting together determines the size and shape of your finished quilt. However, this may be decided by your wishes in the matter with a little careful planning each time. By changing the position of blocks from parallel to diagonal with the edge, the measurement of blocks varies about one third.

Borders are such a potent factor both in adding size and beauty that we are devoting a chapter to them.

For a full bed quilt you will want it not less than 72 inches wide and perhaps never more than 90 inches wide even for a spread. However, many of the old-time quilts used on high four-posters measured full three yards square, but they had to master several feather beds and hide a trundle bed by day beside! Seventy-two is too short for the length of a quilt; even for a closed foot bed it should be a foot longer and for an open foot bed 90 inches is a favorite length. Where one wants a handsome quilt to serve as a top coverlet as we do these days, 99 or even 108 inches is preferred by many. So your blocks whether they be 6 inches square or 18 inches square may be arranged to fit somewhere into this sliding scale.

Size is a matter of taste again. One woman writes that she doesn't want a stingy little quilt that you can see her bed springs under. She had completed a pair of twin spreads in beautychine, and much to her disgust, they were undersize. So we made matched flounces of satine, corded them on at the top and bound their scallops at the bottom which gave both generous size and an air of distinction. Another woman with different taste complains, "My blocks are set together and it looks more like a barn door than a quilt!" From this huge top we subtracted enough blocks to make a pair of boudoir box edge pillows for the head of the bed, and padded tie-on cushions for the bedroom rocker and dressing table chair. You see there is always a remedy, no matter how grievous the wail.

For twin beds 68 inches is a minimum width, although they could be as narrow as 63 for inner quilts where they are for warmth only and not for a top covering. Seventy-two inches is lovely width on a twin size and of course lengths are the same as for wider beds.

BORDERS

THE BORDERS of quilts are seldom given the prominence that they deserve. Too often we say, "I want my quilt about 72 inches wide by 84 long so I'll use blocks 12 inches square, that's 6x7—42 blocks. All right, that's that"; and the quilt may be ever so much work, beautifully done, and yet look disappointingly ordinary when finished. Personally I'd as soon hang my pictures unframed, as to finish my quilts unbordered.

The simplest and often most effective way is to use a wide band of white, say 5 inches wide at the sides by 8 or 9 at the ends. This, beautifully quilted, and bound around the edges with a color repeating from the pattern, is one solution. Color bands, white and two colors from the pattern make a handsome border, especially with mitred corners. Or the wide plain border may have pieced stars in the corners, or repeats of whatever block is used in the quilt center. Very distinguished looking coverlets are achieved by having a center square or oblong closely pieced, like Arabic lattice, Spools, Square and Compass, about a foot smaller than the bed top. Surround this with a 10-inch band of plain for display quilting, then a pieced border repeating the design and a narrow darker border to complete. This takes less blocks and makes a more effective top than when pieced clear to the edges.

Commonest of the pieced borders on old quilts is the "Saw Tooth." This is simply a row of squares, each square made of two triangles, one light and one dark, so placed that the darks all go to the outside and the whites in next the white of the "set." A triangle border in better design is made by using isosceles triangles instead of right triangles; such a cutting unit may be found with the block pattern called "Spider Web." When a white strip is placed between two rows of Saw Teeth, with the dark to both outside edges, the "Double Saw Tooth," a really handsome border, is formed. "Zig-Zag," like the quilt design of that name, is another triangle border; "Flying Geese" or "Wild Goose Chase" yet another. This one takes two sizes of triangles as shown in the block pattern "Wild Goose Chase" and has a decided movement not found in the other staid designs. A border that "stays put" is preferable to one which leads the eye relentlessly on and on. By alternating the colors in each little pieced oblong, as shown in one fourth of "Swastika" one gets a different border entirely, but built on the same two sizes of triangles as used in the "Goose Chase."

Diamond blocks sewed into a strip alternating dark and light make a neat little border, or two rows that lead in different directions and jog the color placing produce a very good one. This plan is sometimes called "Laurel Border" and does look like a laurel wreath when pieced of green and white. One similar to this, with the ends clipped to look even more like leaves, is shown on our original design, the Trumpet Vine. Ribbon border block, one of our hundred and one, is an excellent pieced border to use next a plain one, either around a whole plain center or with a pieced center.

Almost any pieced block can have a special border unit evolved from it which harmonizes with the design—triangle borders exactly suit some, others could use alternate color squares or pin wheels and squares; there is an old-fashioned one called "Tile Border" which is really just little "Necktie" blocks with the center square only in dark or contrasting color. "Spools" also makes a clever patchwork border, as does diagonally placed dark squares, filled in to the outer edges with light triangles either side.

One of the most elaborate quilts that I have ever seen, a real museum piece, has no less than ten borders around a gorgeous applique and embroidered center. The owner calls it "Framed Medallion" and surely it is. One border is a double row of light and dark Zig-Zag so placed as to give a dark ric-rac effect on light, another flanks triangles with diamonds, alternating position each time and meeting in four most precise corners of two diamonds each. There are bands of print between pieced borders, one border is even appliqued and the widest one pieced of eight-pointed stars is about seven inches wide.

A pieced border which scallops is given with the "Friendship Ring" pattern.

Applique borders are more usual on quilts of their kind than pieced ones are on patchwork. There are the scallops that sometimes add onto a straight edge quilt and sometimes match a cut edge. These may run a sequence of color overlays as green for an outer scallop with rose and pink over it for a rose applique. There is a scallop cutting pattern with "Double Irish Cross" which may be extended to become an exact multiple of your quilt edge. If your quilt is 90 inches long the scallop might be 9, 10, or 15 inches, or even 13, by a trifle of manipulating. The scallop itself is often scalloped into little unevennesses, or may drop in a sort of triple curve. These are apt to be rather heavy, awkward looking additions, rather reminiscent of the funeral hearse when ponderous tassels hang between. Sometimes the tops met in a totally inadequate little tulip looking like a crowned tooth, or other times this join was weighted down with princess plumes or great green oak leaves.

A well proportioned scallop, one in keeping with the quilt pattern in daintiness, color, and curve may be the loveliest possible finish for your quilt. One is suggested with the pattern called "Rose Cross." Roses, Fleur-de-lis, leaves, plumes and tassels may be used with the applique scallops, but restraint and a feeling for design are cautioned to mix well with them "before taking."

Most satisfactory of all applique borders, in my opinion, are the running vine types. These may have a stem cut on a continuing "S" shape, or use regulation bias tape which accommodates itself to any curve. On this foundation beautiful borders are builded, with leaves at precise angles, with flowers above the bend or grapes below. Tulips made of three petals and 3 layer roses notched around like a cooky-cutter are favorites in keeping with the antique feeling in appliques. These, with certain buds, big and little, were favorites always.

Usually an applique border is best on an applique quilt, and a pieced one with pieced blocks. I have seen artistic pieced work around applique, especially when there is some piecing in the block, but an ornate vine or scallop border around a homey pieced center is as out of keeping as a massive gold frame on a chaste little etching.

There are original borders on many quilts of later day resulting from women's developed sense of design. An inclosure around angular or erratic forms, such as pieced blocks often are, sustains the whole. I well remember a testy old art teacher's example of that; the question was on rug design, as to what relation the border should bear to the pattern. We students must have all looked blank because he immediately hammered a desk with his cane and queried, "Well, well, if you had a bull in a pasture, should the bull or the fence be stronger?"

So we have designed "strong" borders of twining vines, of little flowers with spreading leaves and such.

On our embroidered flower garden quilt there is a patch picket border, and around the "Farm Life" group of picture patterns a pieced rail fence, which literally holds in their places all the pigs and poultry. This quilt is far from a conventional classic, but for a child, a boy who loves the farm, or even for a man who thinks he does, it will receive more appreciation than a "Wedding Ring"!

For a high four poster, the valance or flounce like they originally used to hide the stored chests or trundle bed beneath, is a finish in keeping. Many well dressed beds choose this fulled finish which adds to the quilted counterpane for beauty's sake. A 3-inch plaited ruffle is lovely on silk quilts or comfortlike puffs. Bound scallops are good, even on wash quilts and some antique quilts as well as quilted white counterpanes boast a fringe.

However the usual final finish to the quilted top is a binding. One yard of material cut on the true bias into strips about 1½ inches wide will bind a straight edge quilt, but allow one half yard more for scallop edge, or if you want less, piecing. This is usually machine stitched around on the wrong side, to bring over the top, crease back to seam and whip down on the front.

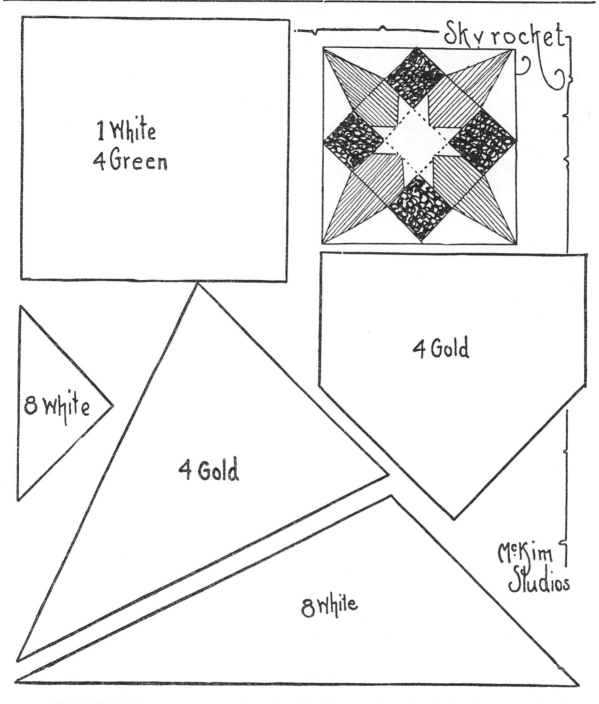

1 White
4 Green

Skyrocket

4 Gold

8 White

4 Gold

8 White

McKim Studios

SKYROCKET

THE Skyrocket is another twelve-inch block particularly adapted for a cushion, using old-fashioned calico prints. These patchwork pillows are just the things for chair seats in an old-time rocker or more scantily padded to tie on to breakfast room chairs for both looks and comfort.

Used in a quilt, this block sets together diagonally with alternate white ones, using half-blocks of the plain to complete. A border of gold and white triangles pieced "zig-zag" makes a fitting finish.

The pattern units above are to be traced onto cardboard, cut carefully and then used to draw around on to cloth. They do not allow for seams, so cut a seam larger and sew back to the pencil line.

In piecing this, the small triangles are first added to the gold blocks to form squares then the center nine-patch made, and the pieced corners added to complete into a really lovely block.

Material estimate: For 25 pieced blocks with the 16 plain blocks, 16 half blocks, (cut diagonally), and 4 corner triangles of the quilt, you will need 2½ yards of gold material, 1¼ yards green and 5¼ yards white.

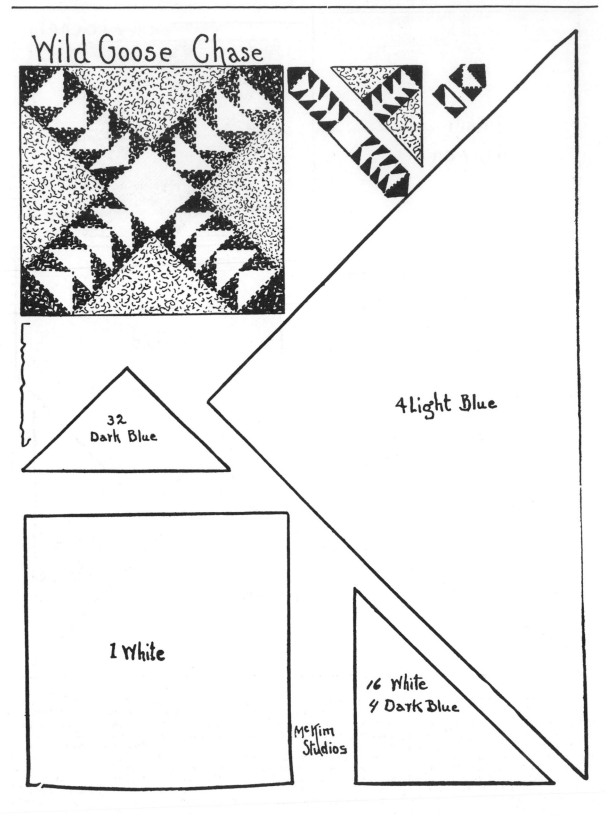

Wild Goose Chase

4 Light Blue

32
Dark Blue

1 White

16 White
4 Dark Blue

McKim
Studios

WILD GOOSE CHASE

WILD GOOSE CHASE is a twelve-inch block, an especial favorite for a little patchwork pillow or chair seat. Or it makes a mighty attractive quilt set together with alternating twelve-inch squares of the light blue, really more effective than with white squares.

Of course other colors than the ones suggested on the pattern may be substituted—any dark and light with white "geese." It pieces in the manner shown in the very small sketches, being mostly a problem of sewing tiny blue triangles on to white ones and joining them properly into strips. A continuing strip of flying geese makes a most charming quilt border.

Add seams to the unit patterns here given. Five blocks wide by six long will make a center 60 by 72 inches. Around this sew a 2-inch border of light blue, then a pieced border of flying geese and a 3-inch border of light blue to finish. Bind in dark blue.

Material estimate: For this plan, allow 2 yards white, 3 yards dark blue, and 5½ yards light blue.

A Spiderweb design could be used on the alternate squares, or a larger pattern like the President's Wreath, as the large light blue triangles of the pieced blocks join the 12-inch plain blue squares.

GRANDMOTHER'S FAN

GRANDMOTHER'S FAN is a good old pattern in which to use silks and woolens. Instead of calling for fancy quilting, too, it is practical when interlined with an old wool blanket and simply tacked at intervals. Each foundation block must be 12 inches square, although the face material does not have to extend under the fan, but a seam. To this foundation block of muslin or whatever is used, are sewed the six assorted color blocks, the first one just basted on with raw edges. The others are sewed joining with edge to edge a seam back and turned over each time into the fan. This method is called making a "pressed quilt."

At the top edge, the raw edge of these pieces is covered by the small black fan, while the wider arc at the base may be hemmed back or finished each time with a scrap of fancy braid. Embroidery stitches often embellished the old-time "Grandmother's Fan." These pattern units do not allow for seams.

This quilt finishes about 72 by 84 inches and includes 42 pieced blocks, 6 blocks wide by 7 blocks long.

Material estimate: You will require 5½ yards of muslin for the twelve-inch foundation blocks, 1 yard black for the corner, and 4½ yards or ¾ yard each of six assorted colors, a total of 11 yards. The fans would be very dainty in rainbow tints, as shading yellow, green, blue, orchid, pink, and orange.

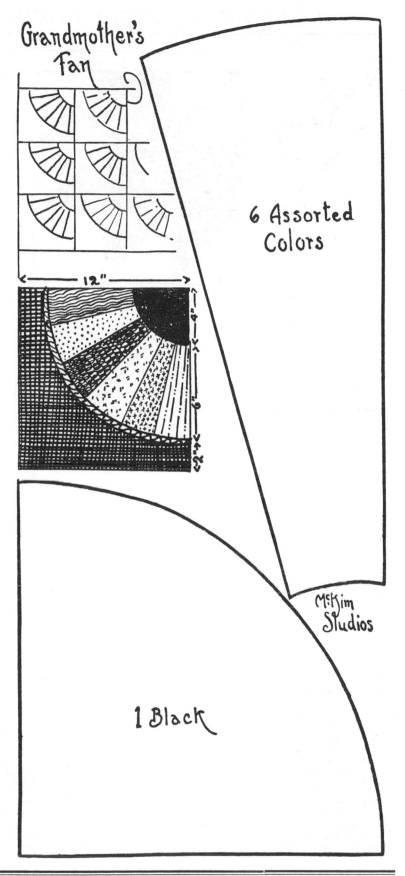

Grandmother's Fan

12"

6 Assorted Colors

McKim Studios

1 Black

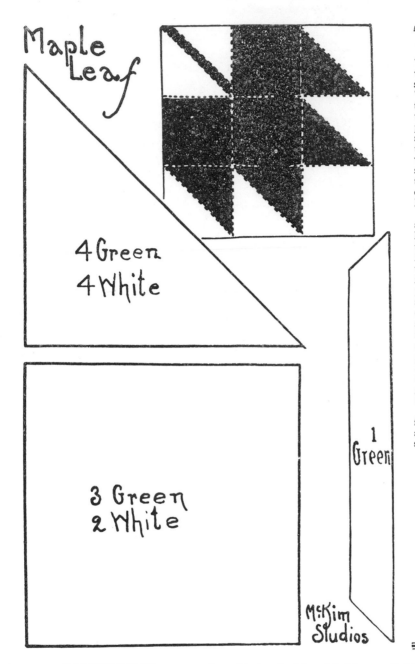

Maple
Leaf

4 Green
4 White

3 Green
2 White

1
Green

McKim
Studios

WEDDING RING

THIS double Wedding Ring quilt should not be attempted by anyone except a real quilt enthusiast. "Believe it or not," the friend from whom we got this pattern boasts 720 small blocks in her counterpane, "mighty nearly all different." That is the unique idea here—no two of the wedge-shaped blocks alike, in close proximity at least. Such a variegated scheme suggests "married life" rather than just the wedding ring, and yet when you see the melon-shaped blocks set together, forming four-patches where they join, you also see large perfect circles overlapping regularly into a really lovely design—wedding rings it seems.

Blocks are made into melon shapes around the pattern marked "1 yellow," half of them with dark blue squares at the ends and half with white. By laying several finished blocks together you will see that a large pillow-shaped block is needed to set them together. This pattern you can readily cut or easier still, simply applique the finished blocks onto white sheeting by turning all outside edges and placing together carefully. For a large quilt, 60 melon-shaped pieces are used and the yardage required is 4 2-3 yards yellow or unbleached for the background or center of block, 6 yards, 1 yard each of 6 variegated colors, 2-3 yard dark blue, and 2-3 yard white.

A Spiderweb design is recommended for the large pillow-shaped white block and flower with leaves to fit the ellipse-shaped block.

MAPLE LEAF

THE Maple Leaf is one of the best examples possible of a charmingly naturalistic pattern from squares and triangles simply placed together. Of course, the applique stem does help, too.

While green is suggested and usually used, there is no reason why gay leaves of yellow, orange, red and brown tones would not make a wonderful quilt. Maple leaves always set together with alternate blocks, check-board fashion, so that the stems all point in one direction diagonally across the quilt in a sort of formal, windblown effect.

Patterns here given are to transfer to cardboard; they do not allow for seams, so cut about a quarter of an inch larger and sew back to your pencil line. Stem does not have to be turned in at ends if it is appliqued onto its small square first, before the block is pieced. This makes a nine inches square block and requires 5½ yards of white with 3 yards of green or autumn tints to complete into a full size coverlet.

The Maple Leaf quilting design from perforated pattern number 330 at 30 cents could be used advantageously on the plain squares.

A border of maple leaf blocks each 9 inches square separated by 3-inch strips would be handsome. This, between 3-inch borders of white, would complete a center five blocks wide by 6 long, into a top about 75 by 84 inches. Bind in color to finish the edge.

Wedding Ring

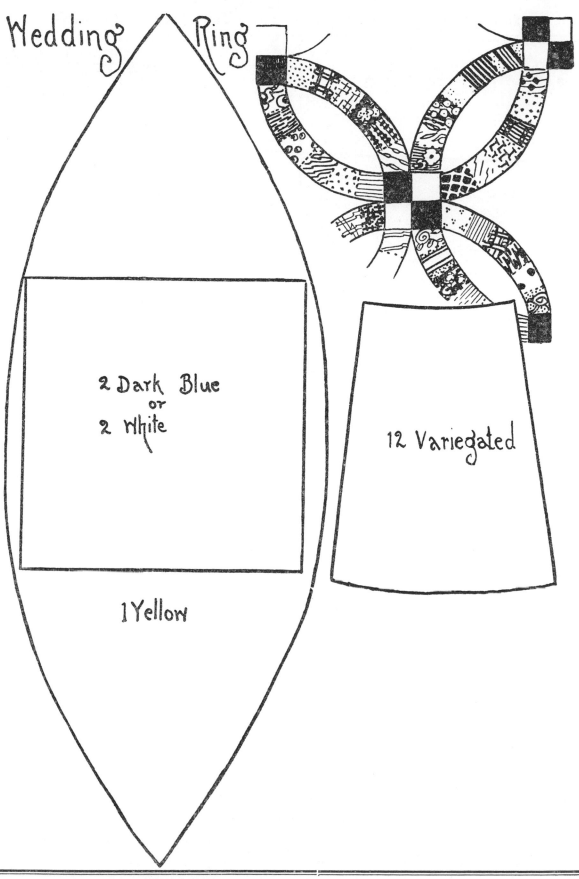

2 Dark Blue
or
2 White

1 Yellow

12 Variegated

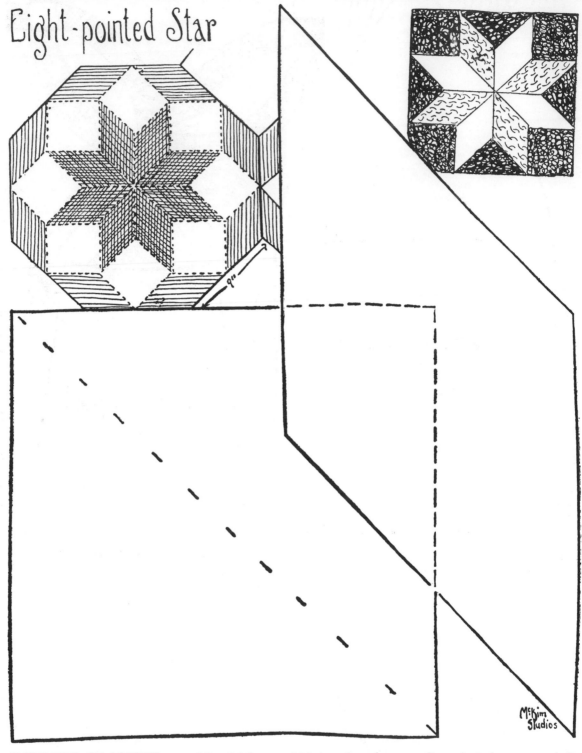

Eight-pointed Star

McKim Studios

ROLLING OR EIGHT-POINTED STAR

THERE are ever so many star quilt blocks of 4, 5, 6 and 8 points. The diamond pattern here given fits together eight times into a perfect eight-pointed one, which is perhaps favorite in the galaxy.

The smaller sketch shows the simplest way of completing it into a block with four squares and four triangles or half squares. But when elaborated with eight squares and then again with eight more diamonds it becomes a glorious affair authentically called "The Rolling Star."

If I were piecing it, I should split each square into two triangles, as suggested on the pattern to simplify the seaming together. Only nine Rolling

Stars with borders of course to add size, are needed to make a quilt.

The Rolling Star blocks finish 21 inches across. You will require 1½ yards of print for the center star diamonds, 3½ yards of plain for the outer diamonds and the six-inch border, and 3½ yards of white.

A Pineapple or 8-inch Feather Circle would quilt nicely on the 9-inch "set" squares.

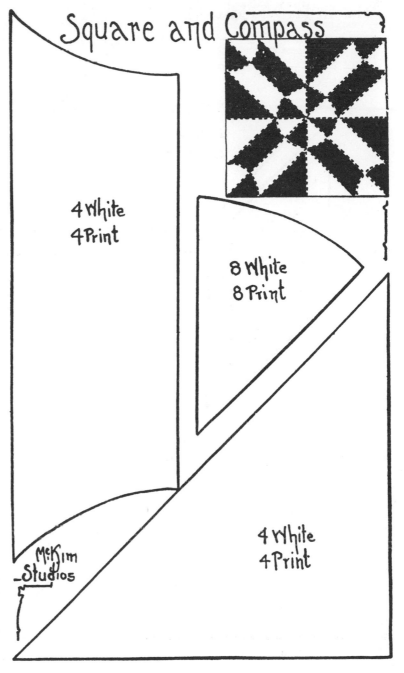

SQUARE AND COMPASS

THE Square and Compass is one of the more intricate quilt designs, and yet there are only three patterns used. As the story comes to us, it was first designed by the wife of a life-saving crew's captain, so to maintain the sea flavor throughout, blue or blue-green with white would make it most nautical. Aside from pointing eight true directions like any real compass should, it some way suggests spars and rudders and propellers. So if you possess that bit of romantic imagination which the quilt originators had, you will surely appreciate the "Square and Compass."

Cardboards are made exactly from the parts here given and traced around, onto the cloth. Cut a seam larger than the penciled part and sew first the triangle block onto the long one, then the "pie-shaped" pieces into the ends to form a larger triangle. This, of course, is half of the small square which in turn is ¼ of a complete block.

Each block will be thirteen inches square, a good size for patchwork pillows, or if making a whole quilt, this pattern uses all pieced blocks which form a continuing and overlapping series of squares and compasses all over the coverlet.

The quilt sets together 6 blocks wide by 6½ blocks long and requires 36 whole blocks and 6 half blocks. It finishes about 78 by 85 inches. Or surround a much smaller center, say 4 by 4½ blocks, with a 5-inch plain band for fancy quilting and a pieced border of half blocks 6½ inches wide to complete.

The more intricate the pattern and the smaller the cut units, the greater the yardage required. For instance, you can make a comfort top 72 by 90 inches from five yards of 36-inch material. But cut it up into squares, or smaller pieces, or yet smaller, and the seams soon take up almost as much as the part that shows. You will need 9 yards for this quilt, 4½ yards of each color.

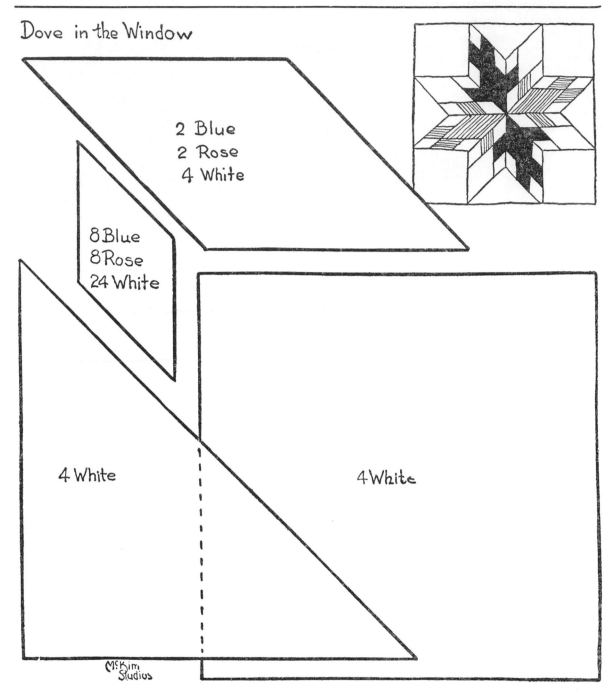

Dove in the Window

2 Blue
2 Rose
4 White

8 Blue
8 Rose
24 White

4 White

4 White

McKim
Studios

DOVE IN THE WINDOW

"DOVE in the Window" is rather an intricate block to piece but a charming and unusual one when done. It finishes about fourteen inches square, suitable size for a patchwork pillow. If used for a whole quilt, set the 25 blocks together with 3-inch strips of pieced sand and white with 3-inch squares of sand color or tiny pieced nine-patches at all intersections.

As with the others in our patchwork series this gives exact size of finished parts; trace these sizes on the wrong side of the cloth, then cut a seam larger sewing back to the line.

The quilt sets together 5 blocks wide by 5 blocks long, with strips 3 inches wide by 14 inches long joined with the squares at the end of these strips. These strips are cut 1⅜ inches, two of sand and one of white to go between them. With seams off from sewing them together, they appear between blocks 3 inches wide. A 3-inch border all around the pieced center may be of the sand color with binding of rose or blue.

Twenty-five pieced blocks, 40 pieced strips and 16 3-inch squares will finish about 82 inches square. Material needed is 1½ yards of rose, 1½ yards blue, 2 yards sand and 4½ yards of white, a total of 9½ yards.

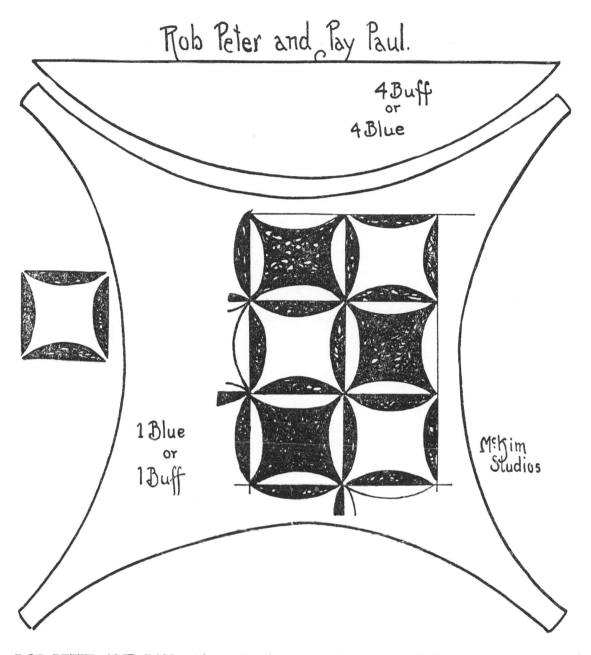

Rob Peter and Pay Paul.

4 Buff
or
4 Blue

1 Blue
or
1 Buff

McKim
Studios

ROB PETER AND PAY PAUL

THIS quilt gets its name from the appearance of the light blocks being cut out to add to the dark, while the dark blocks are trimmed to piece out the light blocks. This procedure is not exactly the case, however, as in reality the blocks must be larger to provide for a seam.

Make cardboard cutting patterns from the sketch given above. These patterns do not allow for seams, so draw on the cloth around the cardboard but cut a seam larger and then sew to the pencil line.

Rob Peter and Pay Paul looks like a series of circles when set together, but the unit block is square, as shown in the small sketch at the left. Of course half of the blocks are made with dark centers and half with light centers surrounded by the darker color. Blue and buff are suggested but any two harmonizing colors make up attractively in this charming, old-fashioned design.

The blocks are a generous 5½ inches square. The quilt may be 14 blocks wide by 15 blocks long to finish about 77 by 83 inches. For the 105 light blocks and 105 dark ones you will need 4½ yards each of a light and dark color. It is equally effective, and less work with a solid center, say 9 by 10 blocks —a wide plain band of the light fancy quilting, a pieced border of blocks, then a narrower border of dark.

This pattern is sometimes called "Orange Peel" and by others "Dolly Madison's Workbox."

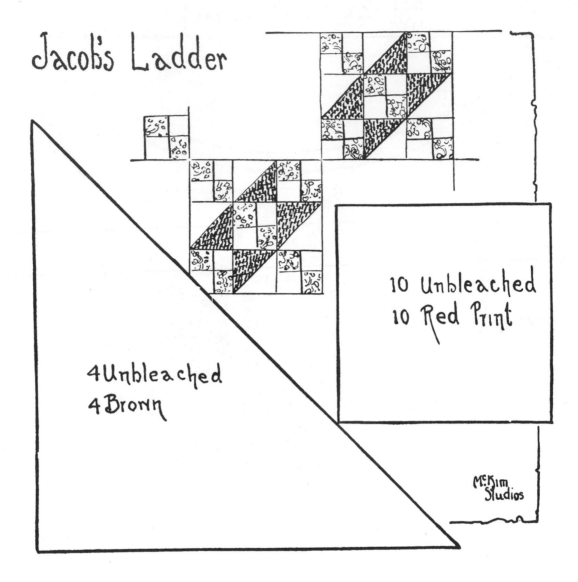

Jacob's Ladder

4 Unbleached
4 Brown

10 Unbleached
10 Red Print

McKim Studios

JACOB'S LADDER

THE Jacob's Ladder block is rather large, 13½ inches square, but it is really composed of nine little pieced blocks, five four-patches and four triangle squares. These nine little patchwork blocks and again the large squares must all be set together so that light squares follow light and dark ones dark, as shown in the sketch. Other-

wise Jacob might yet misstep on a faulty ladder!

The band of four patches set diagonally between dark triangles makes one of those clever little patchwork borders which add so much of well planned beauty to a patchwork quilt. It would finish about 6 inches wide and could be effectively spaced between plain color strips of dark or light.

The quilt sets together with alternate

unbleached blocks, 13 inches square, and is 5 blocks wide by 5 long plus a three-inch border. If thirteen pieced blocks and twelve plain ones are used the quilt will finish about 73 by 73 inches. Material required is 5 yards of unbleached, 1½ yards red print, 1 yard brown and 1 yard extra for the three-inch border.

An Anchor design, slanted all one direction, would be lovely quilted on the large plain squares between "ladders."

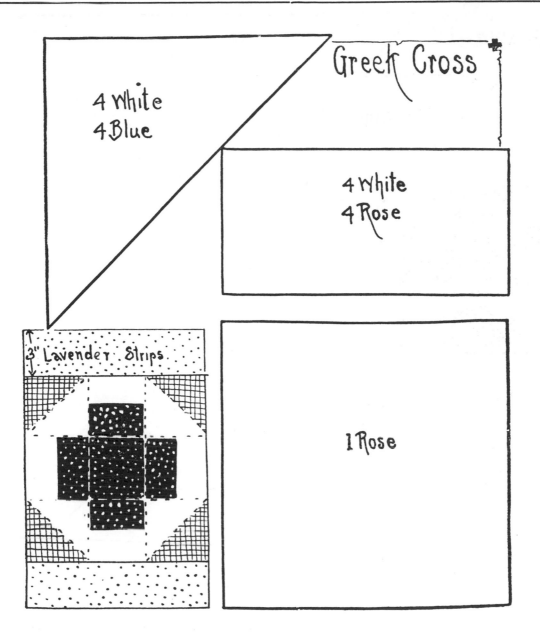

GREEK CROSS

THIS Greek Cross is one of the many variations of nine-patch, that old-time favorite upon which so many little girls have learned the gentle art of stitching. However, Greek Cross is quite an elaborate version, and made up in the analogous color harmony suggested above, three kindred colors in about the same light and dark value, it is a beautifully unusual quilt.

The block is nine inches square and the strips between the blocks are three inches wide. Patterns are made by tracing the ones here given onto cardboard and cutting carefully. These are used to mark around onto your cloth, but cut a seam outside of this line. The pencil line is used to sew to; it marks the size of each finished part.

The quilt includes 49 blocks, 7 wide by 7 long, and sets together with strips 3 inches wide by 9 inches long. Fill in the intersection squares at the end of the strips, when putting together with blue 3-inch squares. Forty-nine pieced blocks, 84 lavender strips, and 36 blue 3-inch squares will finish about 81 by 87 inches if 3-inch strips are added at top and bottom for additional length. You will require 2½ yards of lavender, 2 yards white, 1½ yards blue and 2 yards of rose.

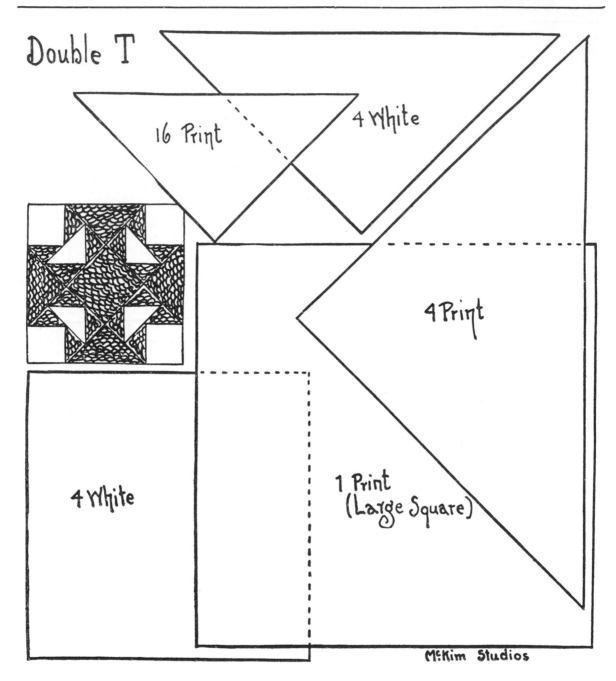

Double T

16 Print

4 White

4 Print

4 White

1 Print
(Large Square)

McKim Studios

DOUBLE T

PICTURING a quilt block is quite a different matter from visualizing a series of blocks set together to form an entire quilt pattern. Double T is rather complete in itself, therefore good for a patchwork pillow, and good size too, as it is twelve inches square. It may set together with alternate plain squares or is especially attractive with three-inch strips of white or harmonizing color between blocks, either continuing in unbroken lattice work or with three-inch squares of the other color at the corners.

Patterns are made by tracing the ones here given onto cardboard and cutting exactly. These do not allow for seams. Draw on your cloth around cardboard, but cut a seam larger, sewing back to the pencil line.

The quilt sets together with 3-inch strips of white intersecting with 3-inch squares of print at all corners. If it is five blocks wide by five long plus the 3-inch strips it will finish 72 by 72 inches. A 3-inch strip may be added at top and bottom for additional length.

Twenty-five pieced blocks, 40 strips 3x12, and 16 3-inch squares will require 4 yards of print material, and 5 yards of white.

QUILTING PATTERNS

OLD-TIME quilting patterns were few compared to the great number of designs for patch-work. About a dozen standard patterns, with their variations completed the list. Here they are: diamonds, shells or scallops, circles, ovals, cables, crescents, stars, hearts; leaves, running vines, tulips, roses, buds; pineapples, harps, birds, baskets, and feathers, feathers, feathers!

The easiest pattern of them all was made of single lines running diagonally across the quilt. Diagonal stitching shows to better advantage than that running parallel with the weave. Too, the cloth is less apt to tear or pull apart than if the quilting lines are run in the same direction as the threads of the fabric.

The single diagonal lines may be made in sets of two and three thus making the patterns called the double and triple diagonals. This is the first step toward ornamentation in quilting. A further step was made when quilting lines crossed to form the diamond, or differently spaced, the "hanging diamond" or the "broken plaid."

You can make any of these designs without a printed pattern adding them to the top after it is stretched firm and smooth in the quilting frame. For straight line quilting you can borrow an idea from the carpenter; use a cord lightly chalked fastening it in place tightly stretched. Let a second person snap the cord, it will fly back making a straight line that can be brushed off when no longer needed. One tradition was that a bride could snap her "Bride's Quilt" but that was all; she was not allowed to quilt it.

Nowadays we use a yardstick or thinner strip that is perfectly straight, marking on either side to fill in such spaces as used to be "string snapped."

In making the more complex designs with loops, circles and segments of circles it is easiest to buy a pattern. But if you try making one yourself use an improvised compass. This requires a pencil, pin and piece of twine. After determining the radius of the circle measure off the same distance along the twine from your pencil. Tie another loop and let the pin serve as the axis from which the circle radiates. A plate or saucer will also do for marking round designs, and one common little pattern is called the "teacup border" where 3-inch circles make a continuing overlap.

An easy way to make the shell pattern is to trace a row of half circles the desired size to a short strip of cardboard. With a pair of sharp pointed scissors cut around the tracing. This scalloped strip can be laid flat on the quilt and traced. One row completed, lay the strip close to the top of the first row, jogging the placing one half unit and repeating to fill any desired area.

Close shell quilting is beautiful either for borders or background spaces. Larger shells make a favorite edge on a quilted puff or comforter and are nearly always used on the silk comfort that scallops around the edge, then reverses the scallop pattern to make the shells face in for half a dozen or more rows.

Both pieced and applique blocks are almost always marked for quilting in lines which parallel their seams. For instance a nine patch block with its finished squares two inches across would be quilted on all nine squares one fourth inch in from all seams. This would mean 9 squares, each 1½ inches across, ½ inch apart at all places. Each alternate plain square might be gorgeous with a small feather circle, a series of crossed lines, a star or pineapple. A pieced "Skyrocket," "Weathervane," or any star block will make a lovely pattern on the reverse side when quilted to follow the seams. So for strength as well as design we retrace the pieced block when quilting it. Some quilters do not draw lines for this but sew along at an even distance, usually ½ or ⅜ inch from the seams.

For exquisite quilts of fine white muslin or sateen, the very careful quilters marked out with a roweled dress-making wheel or by scratching the line with a needle. In fact, the Kentucky quilters make a marking tool by sticking a strong needle into a large cork, leaving the eye end out to mark with. But only a small space may be marked at a time this way as the line disappears soon.

Marking around cardboard or crinoline patterns with a hard lead pencil is an approved method, but the lead must be hard or a soiled, smudgy surrounding will result. Crinoline's advantage for quilting units is that they may be pinned through this stiff, buckram-like cloth to hold even an elaborate design in place while marking.

The stencil type pattern is also used, or cut out parts with an ornate outside. Many, many hours are spent in marking out a quilt—it is indeed a specialized craft by the time honored methods. That is why many of the loveliest old quilting designs have been adapted into wanted sizes and produced in perforated form. With the busy modern woman in mind, patterns simple or elaborate have been made that will stamp an entire top artistically, which means suitably, in an hour or two of time. Almost every cutting pattern has a harmonious quilting design suggested to use with it.

When using perforated patterns it is well to stamp the quilt top on a table before stretching it in the frames, or even to stamp blocks singly before the top is set together. When the women who are to quilt it do the marking out, they usually stamp a "reach" at a time, which is about 12 inches.

The design of your patchwork will largely determine the designs used in quilting. Angles with angles, and curves with curves, does not always hold true as most piecing is angular and much quilting is curves. Large plain blocks make the major demand for ornate quilting, while the converse is comfortingly true. That is if your piecing be elaborate the quilting may, yes, must be **simple**!

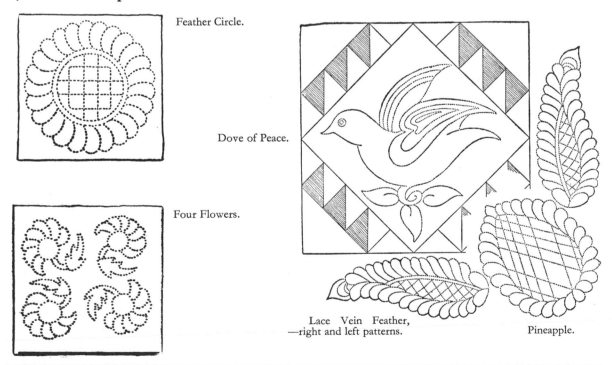

Feather Circle.

Dove of Peace.

Four Flowers.

Lace Vein Feather, —right and left patterns.

Pineapple.

Suggested Perforated Quilting Patterns and Their Use

PERFORATED QUILTING PATTERNS

MARKING a quilt for quilting is more nearly like an artist's job than any step in the making of a quilt. On pieced blocks straight lines, which follow the seams of the patchwork or cross into checkerboard or diamond effects, are usually best. On the alternate plain blocks or strips and on borders the quilting may be as ornate as desired.

Manufacturers have adapted some of the old-time favorite designs in addition to originating new patterns, to fit other space plans. These come on a special tough but transparent paper, the design perforated so that it may be used over and over with stamping paste.

HOW TO STAMP

TO USE stamping paste, wet a piece of cotton lightly with benzine or naphtha, then rub over the paste until the cotton shows color. Place your perforated pattern over your material, smooth side of the pattern up. Hold pattern firmly in place and rub lightly over the design with your cotton. Be careful not to get your cotton too wet. After you have finished using the pattern, pour some benzine freely on a piece of cotton and clean pattern through the perforations thoroughly. This paste will not smear like a pencil or powder but does not remove easily. If stamped lightly the thread should cover it. If you practice first on scrap material you can soon judge how damp to have the cotton, how little paste will transfer, and then there will be no mistakes.

President's Wreath.

Spiderweb.

Plumed Swastika.

Butterfly.

Horn of Plenty.

Wedding Ring Special.

A GROUP OF INTERESTING PERFORATED QUILTING PATTERNS

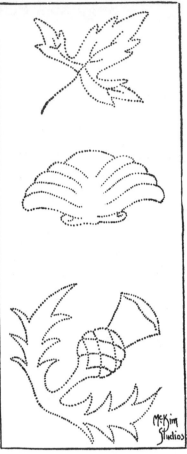

Harp   Feather Circles   Peacock Fan

M APLE LEAF may be used to fill in corners in connection with larger patterns or four on a block. The Shell will make a charming border repeat. Thistle is beautiful for corners, between scallops, for a border, or centered four on a square.

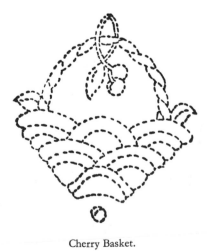

Cherry Basket.

Oak Leaf and Acorn.

Snowflakes.

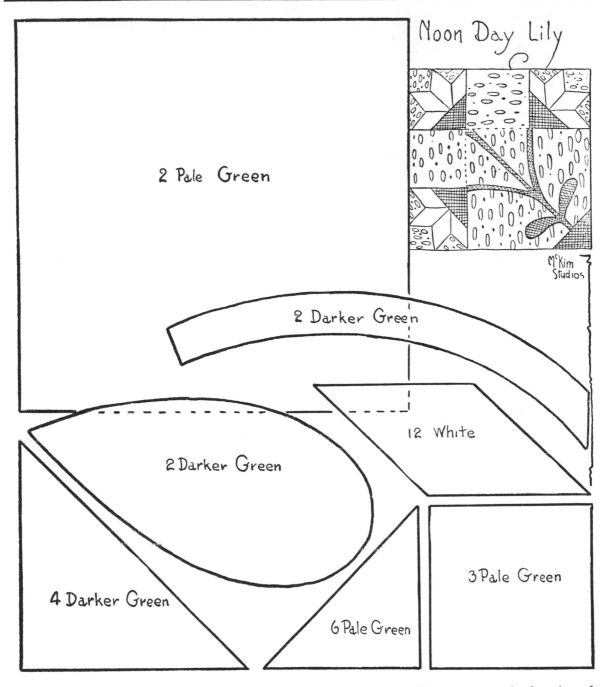

Noon Day Lily

2 Pale Green

2 Darker Green

2 Darker Green

12 White

4 Darker Green

6 Pale Green

3 Pale Green

McKim Studios

NOONDAY LILY

IN THE Noonday Lily block the three small pieced squares are made first, then joined together as shown with two plain blocks of the same size. Then a larger square, the area of four small squares or about 9-inch cuts for the remainder of the block. Onto this applique stems and leaves, and a corner clips off to be replaced with green. The longer straight stem pattern also is not given, but should be about 12 inches long of the darker green.

Twenty-five whole blocks set together diagonally with plain pale green squares of equal size makes a center about 83 inches square. The border of light or darker green could be enhanced by small pieced lily squares appliqued at regular intervals. Borders may be wider at top and bottom to make the quilt longer than wide.

This is an unusual color scheme for the Noonday Lily. Usually the background is white, blossom two shades of some hue such as rose pink, orchid or yellow, with green.

Material Estimate: For the plan described you should allow 6½ yards of pale green, 1½ yards of darker green, and 1 yard of white.

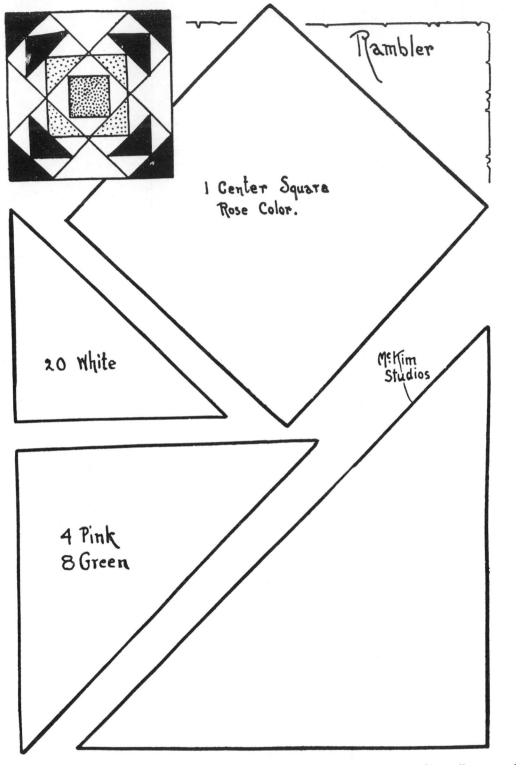

Rambler

1 Center Square
Rose Color.

20 White

4 Pink
8 Green

McKim
Studios

RAMBLER

THIS is the Rambler, an old-fashioned favorite which pieces a block about 12½ inches square, if seams are allowed extra. It is clever either as a patchwork pillow or for a quilt top set together with alternating white blocks, the roses spotting color, and the triangle leaves rambling in formal pattern diagonally across the quilt.

To piece, sew four small white triangles onto the center square of rose. Then piece the four other squares of a pink and a green and four small white

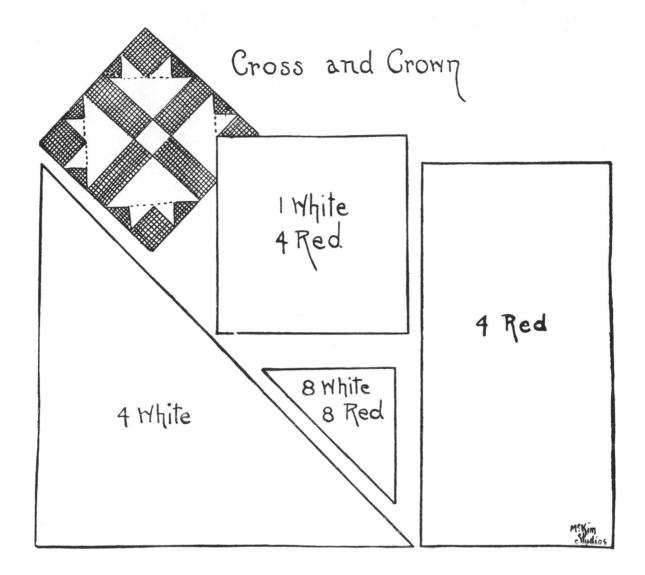

Cross and Crown

1 White
4 Red

4 Red

4 White

8 White
8 Red

McKim Studios

triangles. Complete by making the diagonal center strip and two large corner triangles into the finished square.

Material Estimate: In making this quilt, 21 pieced blocks are set together with 21 plain white 12½-inch squares. Six blocks wide by 7 blocks long finishes about 75 by 87 inches. This quilt requires ¼ yard rose, ½ yard pink, 1 yard green, 6½ yards white, or 8¼ yards in all.

Butterflies would be exquisite on all of the plain squares between ramblers, or a 10-inch Feather Circle would be effective and considerably less work.

CROSS AND CROWN

THIS quaint old pattern with its "firm-in-the-faith" title is really a variation of the lily blocks. They have flowers resembling these "crowns" combined with applique stems, leaves, or perhaps a pieced basket corner as was shown at another time. "Goose Tracks" is also quite similar in pattern but of course less dignified in name! This is one of the more simple quilts to piece, the finished effect varying considerably in relation to the way it is set together.

With red lattice strips joining white squares at the corner the pattern stands out entirely different than when white strips or large squares are used, or again the background may be light with darker design. Allow seams extra; about 3-16 of an inch is right for this on all sides.

If 10-inch blocks set together with white strips 4 by 10 inches and 4-inch red squares, the quilt 6 blocks wide by 7 long will finish about 80 by 90 inches. For the 42 pieced blocks, the 71 white strips, and 30 red squares you will need 3 yards of red material, 2½ yards white, 3 yards white strips and ¾ yard red for squares.

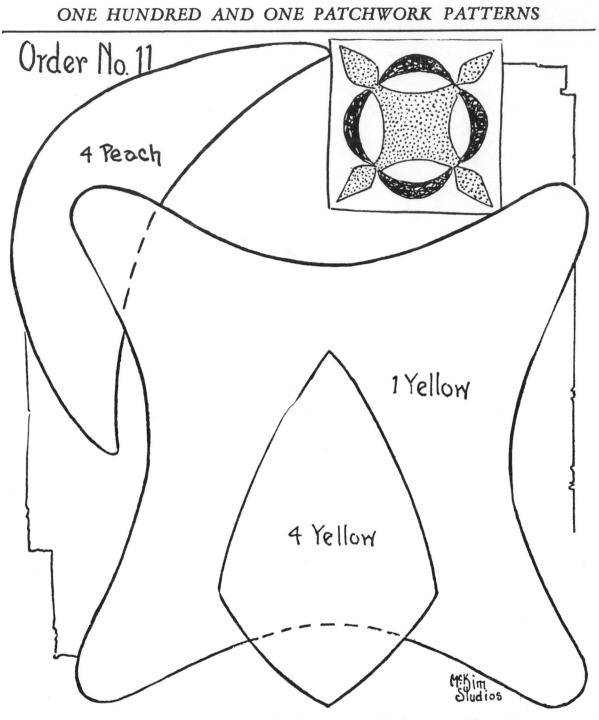

Order No. 11

4 Peach

1 Yellow

4 Yellow

McKim Studios

ORDER NO. 11

THE quilt authorities may identify this pattern as the "Hickory Leaf" and it is doubtless of the stock of that pioneer favorite. But the quilt from which we secured the pattern had such a thrilling history that it deserves its romantic special name—Order No. 11.

A dear old lady in her eighties who was a little girl in Jackson County, Missouri, back in war times, had seen her mother's choice new quilt snatched from the bed by marauders. She carried the memory of its striking pattern in her mind and years later translated it in terms of the white and peach and creamy yellow satine into a quilt, from which we secured this pattern.

A 12-inch square is the background upon which the nine curved sections applique. Patterns here given are the line to crease and baste back to, so cut each unit a seam larger.

The quilt was 7 blocks wide by 8 long and finished about 81 by 92 inches. You will require 6½ yards of white material, 2 yards of yellow and 1¼ yards of peach. This is for a design on every block, but really it would be lovely with less center and a scallop border of the "watermelon" type using an outer scallop of peach with an inner following of yellow.

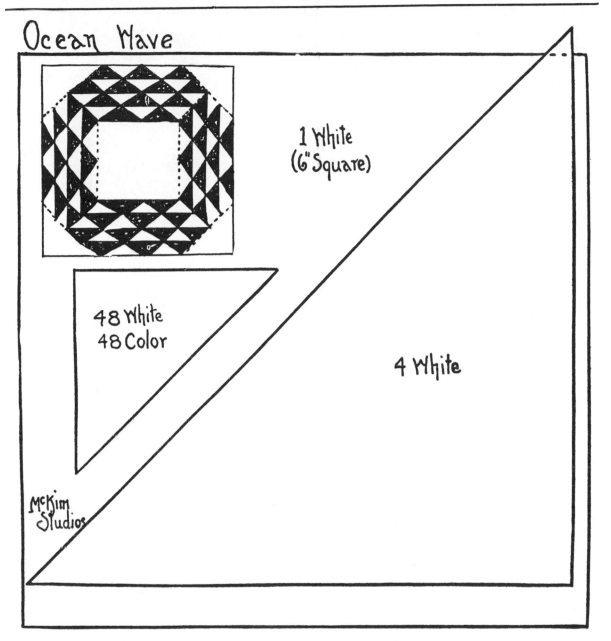

Ocean Wave

1 White
(6" Square)

48 White
48 Color

4 White

McKim
Studios

OCEAN WAVE

THE Ocean Wave is a decided favorite for one who is willing to put considerable piecing into making a lovely quilt. A block is made of four six-sided units of 24 triangles, all made exactly alike, but set together so that the groupings of dark and light triangles alternate as shown in the small sketch. Four of these six-sided units set together as shown in the small diagram finish into a block 18 inches square. These may set together with alternate 18-inch white blocks quilted in matching pattern.

Or, for the really old-time "set" of an Ocean Wave, omit the 4 large white corner triangles.

Join the eight-sided blocks where the large triangles are shown in the sketch, with 6-inch white squares to fill in the center spaces between the blocks. Set the top together in such a way that all six-inch squares will set diagonally on the quilt. This plan makes an overlapping design similar to the double wedding ring. Four blocks wide, with center squares diagonally placed make a top row. An identical four make a second row, but there will appear to be three intermediate blocks with two halves at the sides between these first and second rows.

Material Estimate: In making this quilt, 4 blocks wide by 4½ blocks long, it will finish about 72 by 81 inches. This requires 16 whole pieced blocks, without the four corner triangles and 4 half blocks set together with 6-inch squares and half squares cut diagonally. This requires 3½ yards of print, 5½ yards white. Allow seams extra on all blocks.

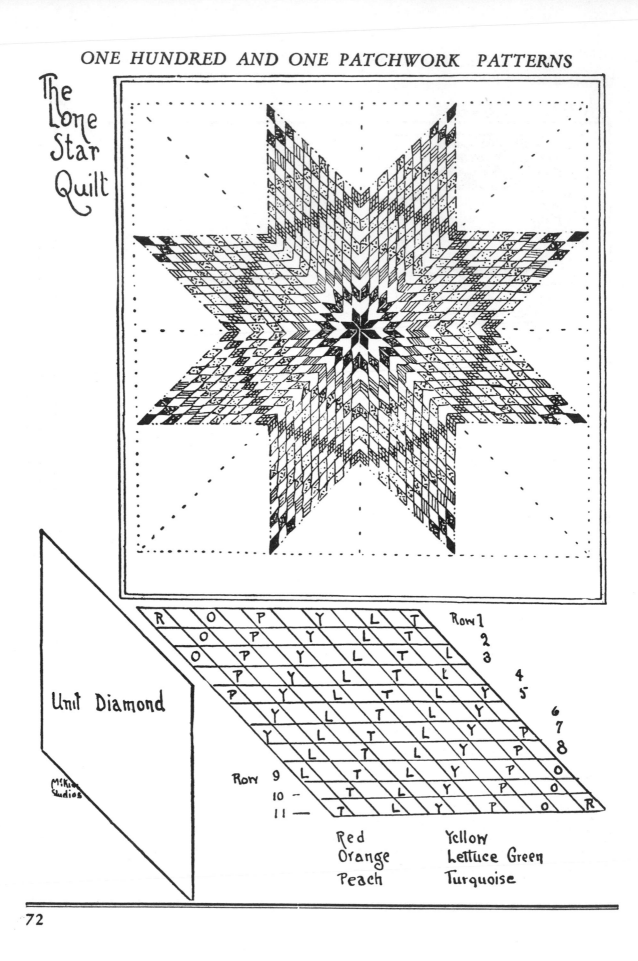

The Lone Star Quilt

Unit Diamond

McKim Studios

Row 1
2
3
4
5
6
7
8

Row 9
10 —
11 —

Red   Yellow
Orange   Lettuce Green
Peach   Turquoise

THE LONE STAR QUILT

LONE STAR, sometimes called "Star of the East" or "Star of Bethlehem," is one of the more ambitious projects in quilt making, and yet the result is so effective that many have completed coverlets of this design. In making any quilt, one should think of the top as a whole; in making a Lone Star it is imperative.

Using the unit diamond to finish the size here given, that is by allowing a seam extra all around, the large star will measure large enough for a very large spread, about 90 inches. Or by cutting the diamonds the pattern size and not allowing extra seams the large star is really a better size, about 68 inches across. Borders may be added in the proportion shown, widest at the bottom to make the quilt longer than wide. You must lay out your color scheme first on a checked diamond as here shown which represents ⅛ of the complete star. Any radiation of color may be planned, either extending out with all different hues or repeating to double back as in the color scheme suggested.

The diamonds are pieced together in rows, the rows then joined with careful corner matching to form the huge diamond, eight of which make the star. Background triangles have to be cut the exact number of inches that your star points finish—about 25 inches in the quilt shown.

For quilting we suggest a large Rising Sun to fill in the squares and half squares.

Material Estimate: The Lone Star quilt requires 4 inches of red, 12 inches orange, 20 inches peach, 28 inches yellow, 36 inches lettuce green, 44 inches turquoise, which is four yards for the colored diamonds; four yards for the white diamonds and 3½ yards for setting together as shown—11½ yards in all.

WIND BLOWN SQUARE

THE Wind Blown Square is a sort of topsy-turvy pattern originally pieced of white with light and dark prints. Of course analogous colors always make lovelier quilts as lavender and violet, buff and apricot, or pink and rose which is suggested. Contrasting colors may also be used as peach and jade green, or yellow with blue-purple.

Material Estimate: In making this quilt, 36 pieced blocks are set together with 36 plain 9-inch blocks, 8 blocks wide by 9 blocks long. This finishes about 72 inches by 81 inches, and requires 1 yard of rose, 1 yard pink, and 5½ yards of white.

The Four Flowers design would quilt beautifully on the alternate plain blocks.

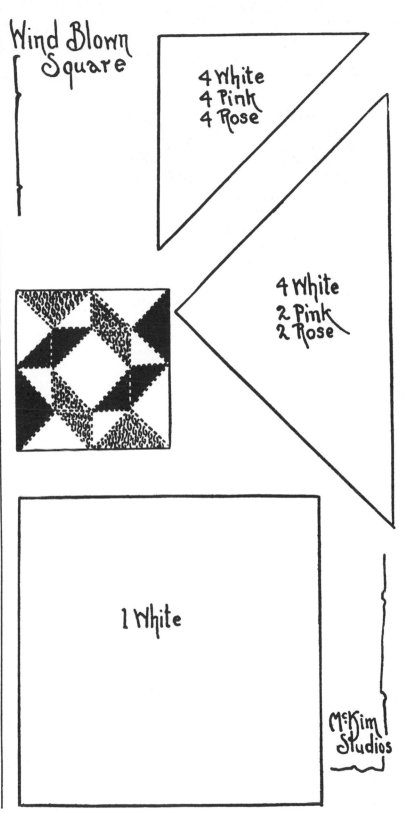

Wind Blown Square

4 White
4 Pink
4 Rose

4 White
2 Pink
2 Rose

1 White

McKim Studios

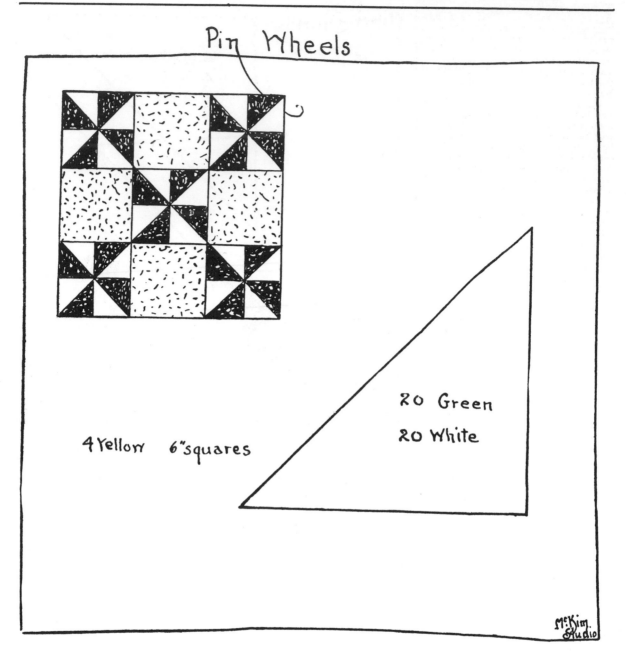

Pin Wheels

4 Yellow 6"squares

20 Green
20 White

McKim Studio

PIN WHEELS

PIN WHEELS with an ancestral name older yet—"Flutter Wheels" —is one of the easiest of all patchworks to make. We remember seeing this motif on "Barbara Fritchie's" quilt in her house at Frederick, Maryland.

The only bit of wisdom to proffer on making this pattern is to cut all triangles on the true diagonal, that is with threads parallel to the two shorter sides each time, and then to not stretch the bias edges in seaming them together.

This may be an all-over pattern or the nine patch unit here shown may be used as a block and set together with lattice strips or plain squares. This is a good design for using scrap material of the children's frocks and rompers— dainty bits of print and plain to commemorate happy days. Seams may or may not be allowed extra. A clever patchwork border to use between plain strips could be composed of little pin wheel squares set diagonally between triangles, like the center band from this block.

Material Estimate: If seams are allowed extra, the blocks will finish 18 inches square—16 blocks set together with 4-inch strips of white, will finish about 84 inches square. This requires 2½ yards of yellow, 2 yards of green, and 4 yards of white, or 8½ yards in all.

A Maple Leaf would be interesting quilted on each 6-inch square, with a narrow Cable on the strips between blocks.

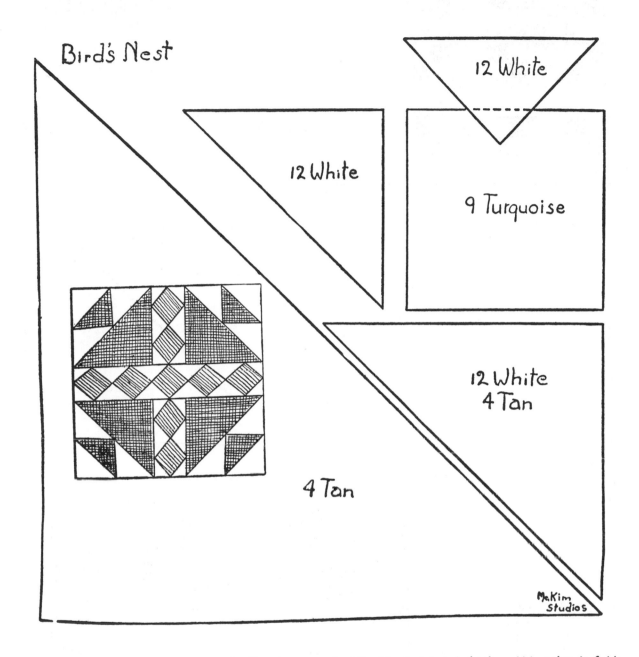

Bird's Nest

12 White

12 White

9 Turquoise

12 White
4 Tan

4 Tan

McKim Studios

BIRD'S NEST

A BIRD'S NEST in soft tan chambray or broadcloth is contrived along modern angles to enclose nine bright blue-green cubist eggs. The whole forms a really lovely block to use in a whole quilt or for a gay little patchwork pillow about 14 inches square. By the way, a boxed edge of the blue squares and white triangles would be a perfect finish for such a pillow. It would even be worth while to piece such a border for the quilt.

Cardboard cutting patterns are made from the 5 here given. Mark around these onto material, but cut a seam larger sewing back to the pencil line.

Material Estimate: This quilt sets together with plain white blocks and a six-inch border which makes it finish about 82 inches square. For the 13 pieced blocks and 12 plain ones and border you will need 1½ yards of tan, ½ yard blue, and 7 yards of white.

A President's Wreath would exactly fit the plain squares and twisted cable border would space beautifully onto the 6-inch plain band.

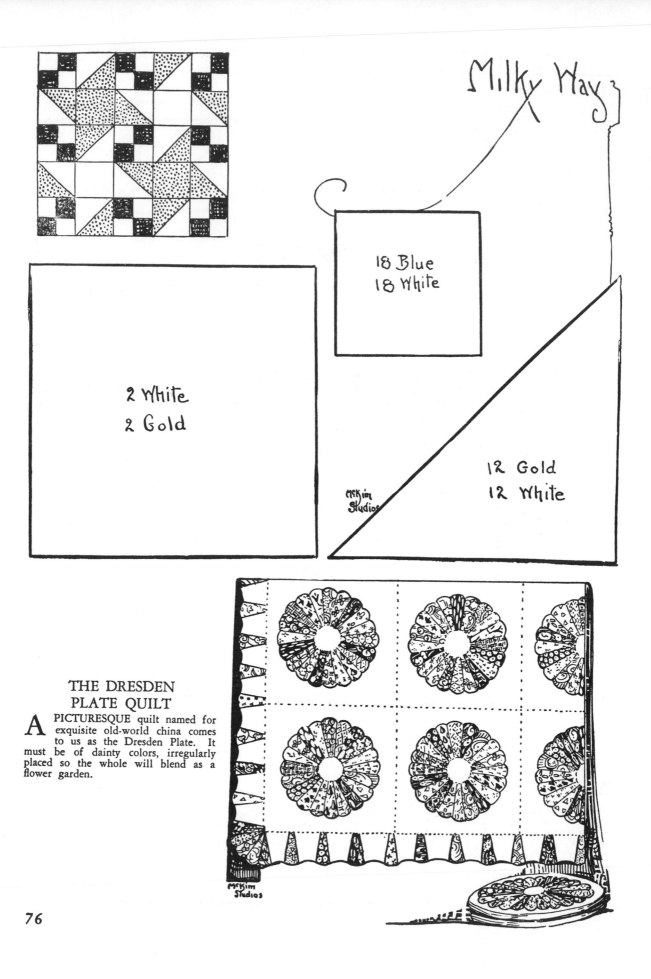

Milky Way

18 Blue
18 White

2 White
2 Gold

12 Gold
12 White

McKim
Studios

THE DRESDEN
PLATE QUILT

A PICTURESQUE quilt named for exquisite old-world china comes to us as the Dresden Plate. It must be of dainty colors, irregularly placed so the whole will blend as a flower garden.

McKim
Studios

MILKY WAY

MILKY WAY is a large block fifteen inches square, or by continuing two more rows top and side it could be made twenty-one inches square. It would make an unusual counterpane by piecing a border all around nine inches wide, which completes the dark and light star, to use with a center of solidly pieced blocks either square or oblong. This would leave a wide plain space of blue or white for quilting between the pieced center and the pieced border.

Milky Way is simple to piece and very effective as well. Seams are not allowed in the sizes here given. This design is even more attractive in very small blocks and of course the two squares and one triangle can easily be reduced in size but kept the same relation to each other.

Material Estimate: To make this quilt with 15-inch blocks as described, make a large pieced center section 30 inches wide by 39 inches long. This is made of four 15-inch blocks, two blocks wide by two blocks long, plus three rows of small 3-inch blocks to make an oblong. Add a 12-inch strip of blue all around. Finish with a pieced border 9 inches wide—2 strips 9 inches wide by 81 inches long and 2 strips 9 inches wide by 54 inches long will be needed for the pieced border. This plan requires 2 yards blue, 3 yards gold, 4 yards of white, or 9 yards in all.

HOLLYHOCK WREATH

ALONG with all the pieced blocks come a few small applique designs. This is a charmingly patterned block using 3 colors on a 16-inch white or unbleached background square. Sixteen squares, either all applique or half of them just plain quilted, make a 64-inch center, which with plain borders is ample for a quilt. There should be a wider border at the bottom both for use and better design.

Cardboard cutting patterns are made exact sizes of the 5 patterns here given. These do not allow for seams, so mark the goods around each pattern, but cut a seam larger and crease back to the pencil line. Baste very carefully, press and whip or blindstitch the units in place. Other plain colors or prints may be used, as lavender, blue or yellow with orange centers, pink with deeper rose or wine red with buff.

This is good size for an odd pillow, using scraps of silk on pongee or black satine.

Material Estimate: In making this quilt 16-inch blocks are set together to make an all-over pattern. Sixteen blocks are required, 4 blocks wide and 4 blocks long, which plus a 6-inch border at top and sides and a 12-inch border at bottom finishes about 76 by 82 inches. This requires ¼ yard coral, 1½ yards apricot, 2¼ yards green and 6½ yards white or unbleached for blocks and border, a total of 10½ yards.

A President's Wreath is most appropriate on the plain squares. Outside of the quilted and appliqued wreaths, fill in with check quilting.

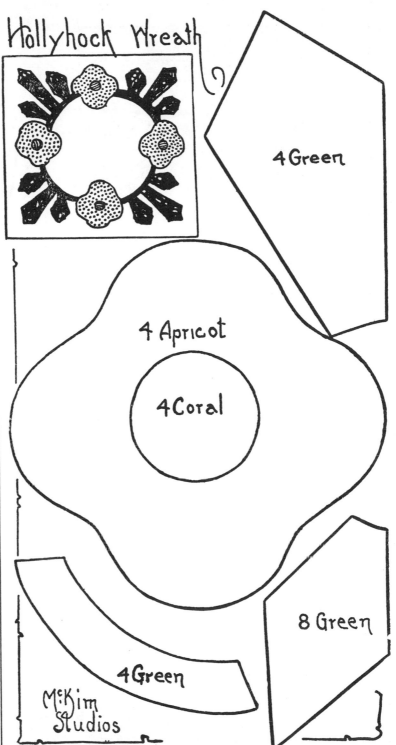

Hollyhock Wreath

4 Green

4 Apricot

4 Coral

4 Green

8 Green

McKim Studios

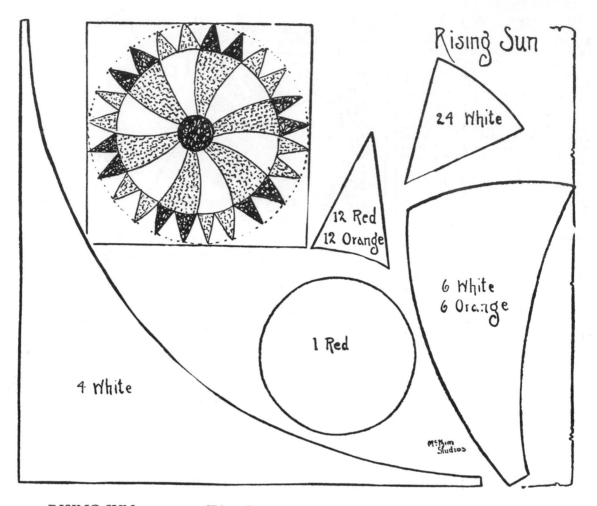

RISING SUN

RISING SUN is an intricate pattern, but not enough so to daunt the quilt maker who aspires to a design that is both lovely and unusual.

The numbers on each pattern are, as always, for one block, although it does sound like a good many this time. Make cardboard cutting patterns, and mark lightly around them onto material. Then cut a seam larger all around and sew back to the pencil lines.

First piece four small triangles, two white and two color, into a block which in turn sews onto the curve block. When 12 of these are pieced sew the long seams which make it into a wheel. The "hub" is gathered into a crease around and appliqued on to finish. Thus this whole wheel or sun, may either be appliqued onto a 12-inch square or pieced in with the four white corner blocks as shown in the pattern. Flame red and orange with white, unbleached or yellow, makes a stunning counterpane from this pattern.

This quilt sets together with alternate white blocks, and contains 23 pieced blocks and 28 plain ones, that is 7 blocks long by 8 wide, finishing about 77 by 88 inches. You will need ½ yard of red, 2 yards of orange, and 6½ yards of white.

AN APPLIQUE RISING SUN

THERE are different versions of the Rising Sun, and the blocks of the one pictured here are to be appliqued onto 18-inch white squares. Thirteen complete applique blocks, alternated with twelve 18-inch white blocks, will make a 90-inch quilt.

This makes a charming large pillow to finish round or square.

QUILTING THE QUILT

WE HAVE carried our story of quilt information through several chapters to help you decide on material, and patterns for piecing and quilting. We have told you how to cut and make up the blocks, and fit them together into a top. That is as far as most modern quilt makers care to go. It is usually the wisest thing here to call upon a professional quilter or your church "aid society" to complete the task—especially if you are inexperienced and the quilt top handsome. It is customary for the owner to furnish lining, cotton bat and thread. Usually the workers mark and quilt them, charging varying amounts in different localities and dependent on the local demand for such work, skill of quilting and the simplicity or elaborateness of designs used. We have known quilters to charge as little as 75 cents for a spool or as much as $5.00. This charge is based on the staple 100-yard spool. Number 50 white is the standard for ordinary materials, although some prefer number 60 or even 70 thread for use on fine cloth such as light satines.

Quilters always have their own collection of quilting patterns from which they evolve the right fill-in for every space, block patterns, borders, and little leaves, hearts or flowers for too wide spaced corners. However, many women of today with their artistic tendencies are using perforated patterns to stamp their own, rather than trust this most important part to the vagaries and whims of some dear old lady who marks out according to the same ideas she has had on all the quilts she has ever done. Besides, it is quite possible to get quilters who can quilt, but will not attempt the marking out. You see that part is apt to be a monopoly in the aid society. Sister Markham does all of that with a high hand and flourish, while the timid Sewell sisters quilt to perfection, but daren't trust their hands at the "art part." Remember that the section quilted around stands up, while the stitched part is held close. For instance in the Lone Star, we quilt on each tiny white diamond, and each colored diamond between puffs up.

"APARTMENT QUILTING"

Maybe this should be "compartment" quilting, but still it was originated for the woman who lives in tiny rooms, efficiency all over, even to finishing her full-sized quilt therein, to its last lovely stitch. This may be done in an apartment that can't accommodate a large picture frame, to say nothing of quilting frames! One young thing wrote, "We even have collapsible tooth brushes, and yet, I am quilting mine own quilt."

The secret is this, quilt the blocks separately, then set them together—a "makeshift," says grandmother with a sniff, "about as backwards as pickin' a chicken after it's baked." But oh, the modern methods we love, the jolly substitutions and short cuts that leave us time and energy for recreations like quilt making. So after the blocks are pieced, and the plain squares stamped for quilting we may cut a back and interlining the same size. Spread them smoothly on a table and baste around and through rather firmly. Then you may quilt them on the table, or on your lap, taking even stitches which go through the entire thickness. Some quilt a fourth of the quilt this way, or eighths, or single blocks. The quilted sections are joined by sewing top parts with a running stitch on the wrong side. Then smooth the interlinings of cotton to overlap about ¼ inch, and sew back sections together with a blind stitch. The quilting is then continued along the join line.

Bias tape in white or a color may be used to cover all seams on the back, making a pattern of squares over it all.

PUTTING INTO THE FRAMES

The authentic way to quilt is to have a large frame into which the whole coverlet is stretched. The frame itself is so simply constructed that every household used to have its own. Four smoothed pine strips 2 inches wide by ¾ inch or 1 inch thick are cut in two lengths. Two long ones are possibly 9 feet long while the width pair may be 90 inches or only four feet. This half width frame means that you can put only half of the quilt in at a time; it saves room, but may sacrifice some in quilting smoothness. Round pieces are excellent for these side pieces, especially when there are accompanying uprights with holes bored to fit which makes the frame rather like a table. Clamps are preferred to bolts for holding the corners securely.

The side bars of the quilting frames should have a fold of ticking or heavy muslin closely tacked their entire length. Pin or baste the quilt lining to these so it will not sag during the days of work to come, one side to each bar. If using the narrow width frame, roll up the extra length at one end; stretch and secure the corners firmly. A lining is better cut several inches larger than the quilts' top as it may become frayed during this part of its useful history. Next the cotton bat is carefully unfolded and spread, and the top placed even more gently over this. Its edges are basted to the edge of the lining at the sides with perhaps a pinned on strip to wrap over the end for perfect smoothness. This is a step which requires precision, and discouragingly shows up any undue fullness or tightness that has occurred in your piecing. However, puffs will quilt down considerably. We saw a "Lone Star" that breezed up like a circus tent, quilt down to satisfaction.

QUILTING

Telling you how to quilt is almost as impossible to write in words as to describe an accordion without moving your hands. One quilter says use a short needle, another holds out for a long needle, nicely curved! After trying it and observing experts it seems to me that the trick is in sewing clear around and back again like your hand could roll about the small curved units, sort of a standing on your head effect. Aye, this is the rub that may keep the quilts of today from really rivaling the ones of yester-year. It is difficult to take small, even stitches, through three thicknesses, especially as one of these is rather heavy cotton. But the running stitches must be even, must go clear through each time, and should be small. The position is rather awkward and tiring to one unaccustomed in the art. The left hand is held under the work, although sometimes it is the right hand under, as many expert quilters get ambi-dextrous. While some can quilt around and towards themselves, decidedly right-handed folks fasten the thread oftener, and always work from right to left.

No matter how beautifully you tat, embroider, play the mandolin or paint china—your first quilting will not be expert; this takes much experience and the novice cannot hope to acquire speed or perfection on her first quilt.

If you try quilting continuously for several hours your fingers are apt to become very sore. A remedy for this is to dip them in hot alum water which toughens the membrane. Thread pulled across the upper side of the right little finger often causes a blister. One way to avoid this is to wear a rubber stall over your finger, which protects it from blisters and bruises. One can only reach about a foot over the side of the frame. When you have finished some twelve inches roll up the quilt. Another section is then unrolled. This quilting and rolling and unrolling is continued until the quilt is finished.

It is then taken from the frame and usually the edges bound with a bias band of material, either white or of the predominating color used in the quilt. This binding should be cut about an inch or an inch and a half wide. It is usually machine stitched on one side of the quilt then turned over and whipped down with small stitches.

BLAZING STAR

THE Blazing Star is a glorious quilt in yellow and orange tones. Finishing with 2 two-inch strips it makes a top 80 inches wide by 92 long. Without border, the quilt is right for a twin bed, or border strips in white and yellow may be made.

IRISH CHAIN QUILT

THIS double Irish Chain has a beautiful apple green tint for the body of the quilt, with white chains centered by a dark green one patterning it all over. This finishes about 90 inches square with the white border.

ROSE OF SHARON

ROSE OF SHARON, the "Bride's quilt" of our fore-mothers finishes 87 inches wide by 93 inches long. Nine large applique blocks and three half blocks, together with the plain white squares for quilting, and a colored scallop border make this top.

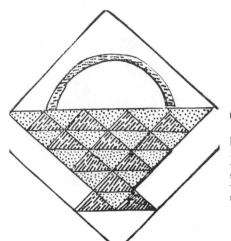

CHERRY BASKET QUILT

CHERRY BASKET is among the most charming of old-time favorites, and this version of pieced basket with applique handle is particularly quaint. It may be developed from the pattern in any color plan, but old-time calico prints, red and yellow sprigged with a fine unbleached, are exactly suitable. Blocks finish 12 inches square.

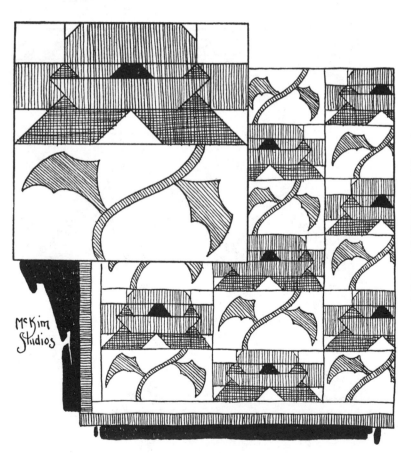

ORIENTAL POPPY

ONE woman said, "Before I catch the quilt fever, I'll have to see a pattern that's entirely different and stunningly beautiful!" The Oriental Poppy is in answer, and beside filling those requirements it is really quite simple to make. The pieced poppy is all straight sewing, the sort that may be run up on the sewing machine, while the bottom half of the block has two leaves and a stem that whips down by hand.

The original was gorgeous in two values of red, a flame and a scarlet, with the flower center of black, boilproof of course, and green applique.

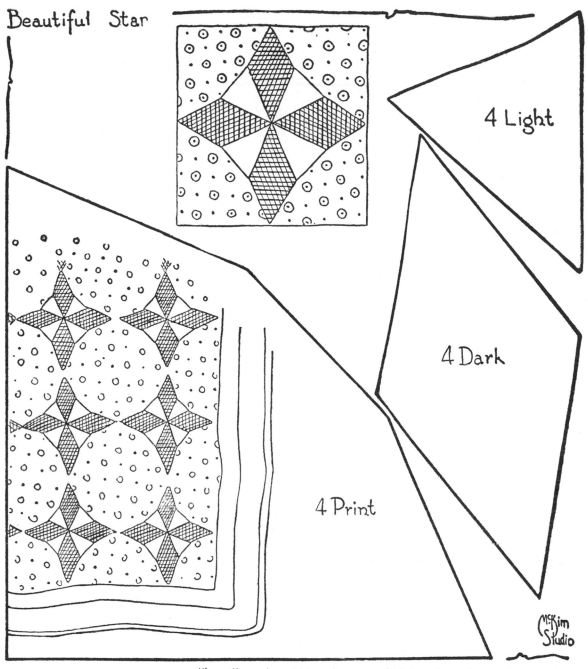

Beautiful Star

4 Light

4 Dark

4 Print

McKim Studio

BEAUTIFUL STAR

VARIETY is truly unlimited in the field of quilts and quilt making. That is one secret of the quilt fascination which charms from generation to generation. So in the quilt pattern above, "Beautiful Star," its name is not its chief claim to distinction, but the beauty of an all-over pattern, that particular "set" which requires no strips or plain squares. It is pieced in a chintz-like calico print which makes part of the block and yet appears to set all blocks together.

The block itself is 10 inches square, not as simple as some to piece, and yet when a yellow oil print combines with dull red and "unbleached" in the blocks it makes a coverlet well worth working.

Materials Estimate: In making this quilt, 10 inch squares are set together to make an all-over pattern. Fifty-six blocks are required, 7 blocks wide by 8 long, which, plus a 2-inch border of light color and one of print will finish the quilt about 78 by 88 inches. This requires 5 yards of print, 2 yards of dark and 2 yards of light for making the border, 9 yards in all, which may allow enough for binding.

The Maple Leaf, Shell, and Thistle designs could be used to good advantage in stamping the blocks singly for quilting, or the Snowflakes or Flowers after four blocks are joined. The pieced star quilts on the seam lines.

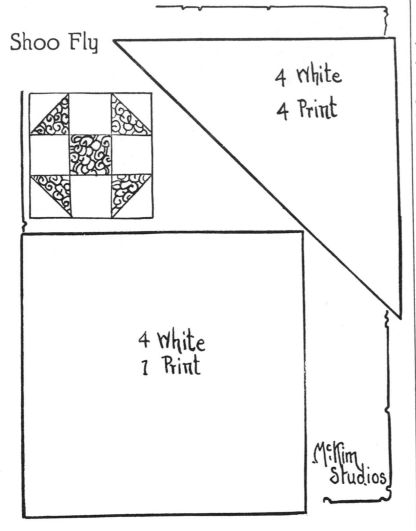

Shoo Fly

4 White
4 Print

4 White
1 Print

McKim
Studios

SHOO FLY

AS SHOO FLY is one of the simplest of old-fashioned patchworks, both to cut and to piece, it would be good choice for one on which a little girl could learn sewing. Bits of her frocks and aprons with perhaps those of her youthful chums, too, would make the blocks doubly interesting.

Patterns are cut from cardboard like the ones printed here, but the cloth could be cut 3-16 or a quarter of an inch larger all around to allow for seams. They then make a block 9 inches square which may be set together with 3-inch strips of white or some one color such as a blue calico print into a clever quilt top.

Materials Estimate: If using light blue for stripping and border with pink print and white blocks, allow about 4 yards blue, 2½ of white and 2 of pink print. This will total 8½ yards.

Quilting suggestion: 8-inch Feather Circle.

BASKET OF ORANGES

BASKET quilts are always endowed with a quaint charm that assures their popularity. There is the "Cherry Basket" which really shows no cherries, the "Grape Basket" sometimes called "Basket of Chips," and the Fruit Basket. There are numerous flower pot and basket designs with both pieced and applique posies above. But the "Basket of Oranges" with its naturalistic fruit and leaves atop a patchwork basket is especially charming.

If seams are added to the marking units here given, a block will finish about 10½ inches square, right size for one of those cunning little tuck in pillows, or a border may be added for size. The cutting patterns here given really piece only the bottom half of the blocks; the large top triangle upon which the appliques place will be identical in size with your pieced half. Allow 3-16-inch seam extra on all applique parts, also.

Materials Estimate: When set together on diagonal with plain unbleached blocks this takes 25 pieced 10½-inch square blocks, 16 plain blocks, 16 plain half-blocks (cut diagonally) and 4 plain quarter-blocks for the corners. It requires ¾ yard orange, 2 yards turquoise, 1 yard green and 5½ yards unbleached or a total of 9¼ yards. The quilt top finishes about 75x75 inches, and extra borders may be added top and bottom for additional length.

One of those delightful "Running Vine" borders, most beautiful of the applique frames, would be wonderful on this quilt. The background could be about 10 inches wide, cut plain or shallow scalloped. On this a continuing S curved vine made of green bias fold with leaves to match, oranges slightly smaller than those in the baskets, and grapes cut the size of a quarter in turquoise.

A simpler border could be pieced from white and turquoise triangles and bordered with bands of green with an orange binding at the outside. Material estimate does not include borders.

The Cherry Basket quilting pattern is charming with this pattern, on the alternate plain squares.

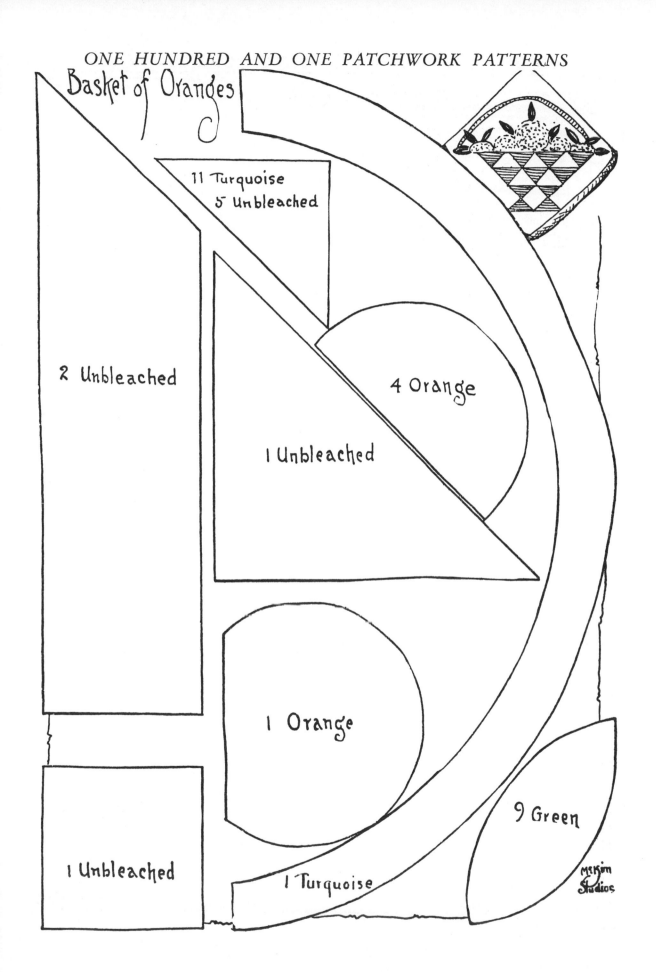

Basket of Oranges

11 Turquoise
5 Unbleached

2 Unbleached

1 Unbleached

4 Orange

1 Orange

9 Green

1 Unbleached

1 Turquoise

McKim
Studios

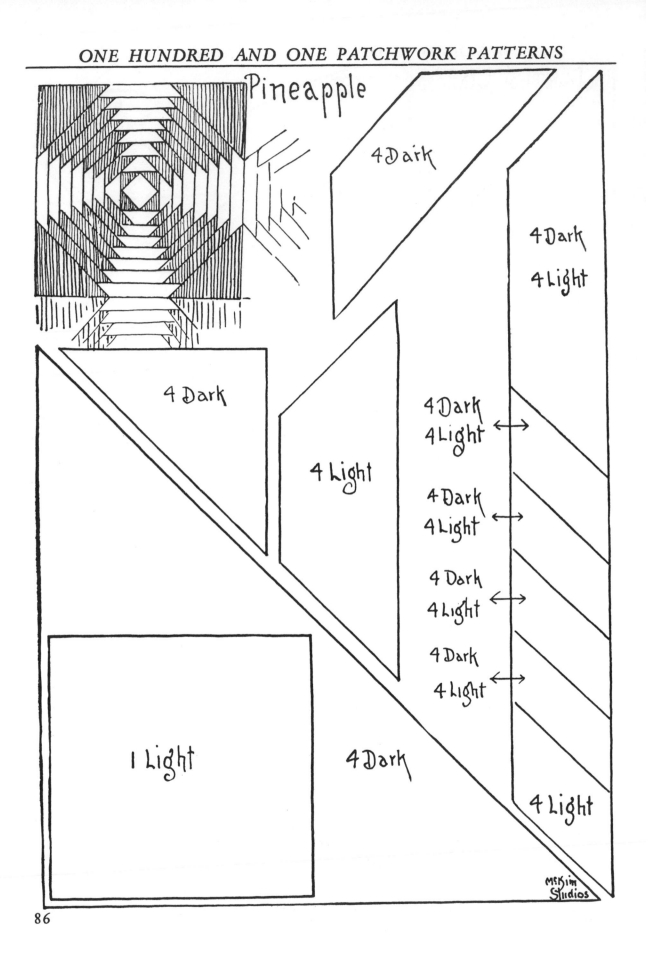

Pineapple

4 Dark

4 Dark
4 Light

4 Dark

4 Light

4 Dark
4 Light

4 Dark
4 Light

4 Dark
4 Light

4 Dark
4 Light

1 Light

4 Dark

4 Light

McKim Studios

PINEAPPLE

THIS very lovely old quilt design, sometimes known as "Washington Pavement" is not nearly so intricate to make as you might imagine. The cutting is especially important as it takes so many even width strips, all with exact 45 degree angles at the ends. But the sewing is straight seams such as may be run on the machine. The pattern may or may not allow for seams, depending on the finished size of each block.

It is suggested for an all-over pattern. One of the most exquisite quilts we have ever seen was this pineapple cut small and done of all gorgeous bits of silk, working from very light center such as lemon yellow, shell pink or ivory through varying values of light to dark with dark green, brown, wine red and even black for the large corner triangles. These corners each boasted a bit of silken embroidery, thus using odd scraps of floss with the old neckties, velvets, brocades, etc.

This may also be a wash material quilt of scraps, each block of white and some one print, or running the sequence of color values from light to dark each time.

The blocks finish about 18 inches square, four blocks wide by 4½ blocks long would be good proportion, and two complete finished blocks could be cut in half if the seams were machine done.

Some women prefer to build this sort of block on a foundation of flour sack or such material, starting at the center square, of course, and covering to turn back each time. This way the center square is basted into position with raw edges left all around. The four dark triangles seam to turn back one over each side, with raw edges again to their outsides. Press, and repeat with the four shortest light blocks, etc. In quilt parlance this sort of technique was known as making a "pressed quilt."

A full sized Pineapple quilt will take about ten yards of cloth.

In quilting a design of this sort best results are obtained by stitching along the seams—say 3-8 of an inch either side of all piecing seams. Where the four triangles come together a design may be quilted, such as Thistles, Shells or Maple Leaves.

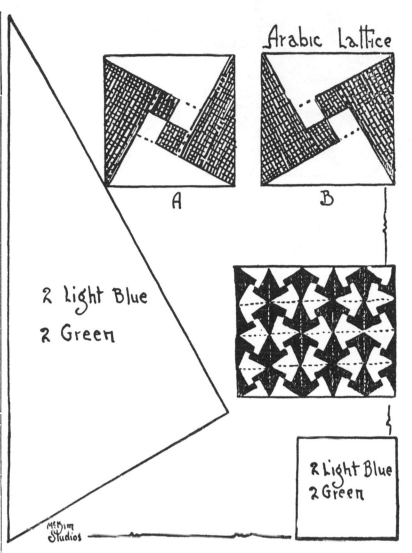

ARABIC LATTICE

FOR those who want something different again and who do not mind fitting around corners to achieve the results we suggest "Arabic Lattice." The originator of this old pattern must have had a flair for the romantic as witnessed by the name as well as an aptitude for work, as the little blocks are really difficult to piece.

Each finishes 5½ inches square if seams are allowed extra and they must be pieced in A and B style to set together alternately for the all-over pattern. These blocks in a continuing row turn an intriguing corner as well as making a single repeat border that is most effective.

A pieced center of 30 or 42 little blocks, within a wide band of plain color for fancy quilting, then a pieced border and a plain to finish would make a stunning quilt.

Material Estimate: Forty-two of the 5½-inch blocks would finish into a center about 33x38 inches—6 blocks wide by 7 long. This center plus a 12-inch border of light blue, then a 5½-inch pieced border, and last a 3-inch border of green, will make the completed quilt top 74x79 inches. This requires 5 yards of light blue and 4½ yards of green, or a total of 9½ yards of material.

For the intricately pieced center, lay out in straight lines for quilting and repeat the Tulip or Snowflakes designs for quilting the wide plain border.

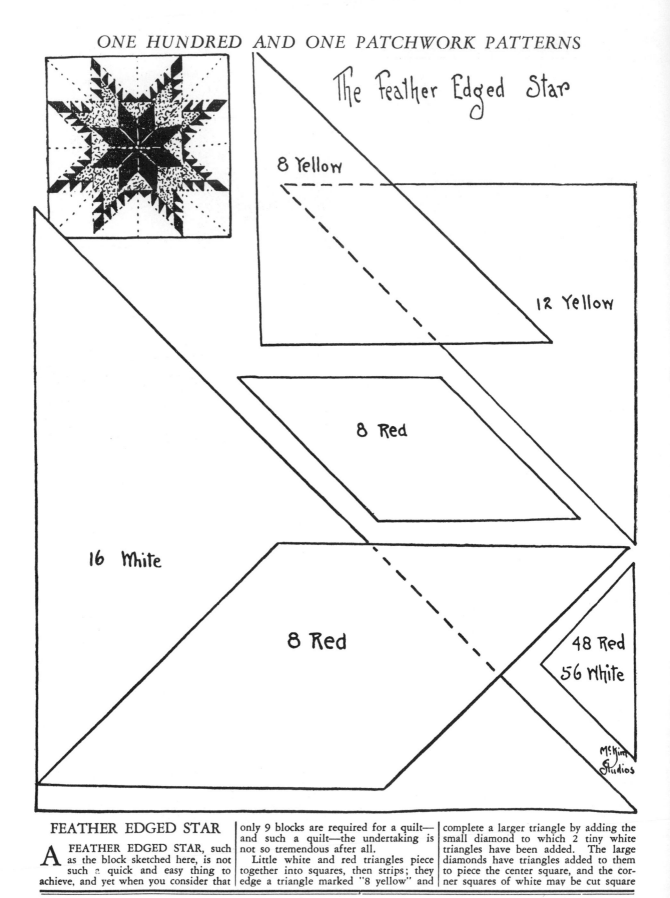

The Feather Edged Star

8 Yellow

12 Yellow

8 Red

16 White

8 Red

48 Red
56 White

McKim Studios

FEATHER EDGED STAR

A FEATHER EDGED STAR, such as the block sketched here, is not such a quick and easy thing to achieve, and yet when you consider that only 9 blocks are required for a quilt—and such a quilt—the undertaking is not so tremendous after all.

Little white and red triangles piece together into squares, then strips; they edge a triangle marked "8 yellow" and complete a larger triangle by adding the small diamond to which 2 tiny white triangles have been added. The large diamonds have triangles added to them to piece the center square, and the corner squares of white may be cut square

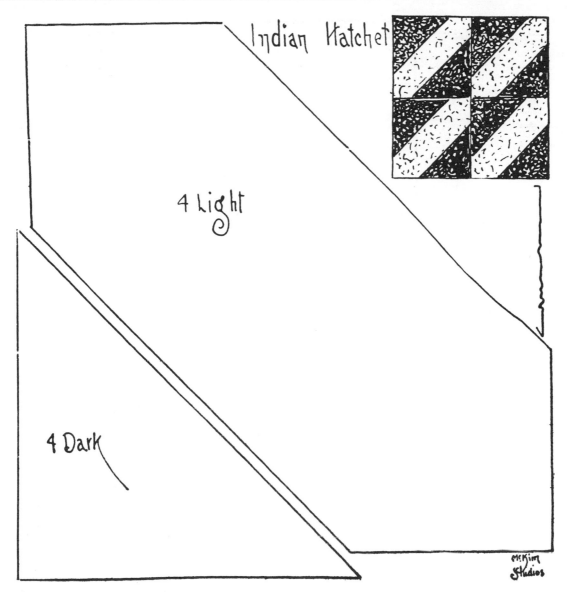

Indian Hatchet

4 Light

4 Dark

McKim Studios

instead of pieced from triangles if the star is worked up in this sequence.

Seams are not allowed. The borders of plain which are added to make the complete top the desired size are often wider top and bottom than side borders, so the finished top may be longer than wide.

Materials Estimate: Nine of the 25-inch blocks finish into a quilt top about 75x75 inches square, 3 blocks wide by 3 long. It requires 4 yards white, 4 yards red, and 2 yards of yellow, or a total of 10 yards of material. This does not include border. In quilting an all pieced design, like this, simply follow the sewing seams. Small feather circle might be transferred onto the center star, and cable or feather band borders for edge bands.

INDIAN HATCHET

WARLIKE and treacherous as the name may sound, we guarantee this to be one of the most peacefully simple little blocks to put together of all the old-time patterns. Many a little girl has learned to sew on Indian Hatchet blocks, although a mother perhaps supervised the cutting out.

This should be accurately on the true bias with threads running parallel to the right angle sides. Seams may or may not be allowed additional to the sizes here given. Some women like their cardboard patterns to make the line upon which to cut, while others prefer to mark around, cut a seam larger, then sew back to this line. If the pencil lines are on the wrong side of cloth, when the right sides face together to seam, this pencil line assures that accuracy which is the prime requisite of "piecing."

Material Estimate: Allow extra for seams to make these blocks 11 inches square. Twenty-eight pieced blocks set together with alternate plain squares make a quilt top about 77x88 inches, 7 blocks wide by 8 long. It requires 3 1-3 yards light, 2 yards dark, and 2 2-3 yards white for plain blocks, a total of 8 yards.

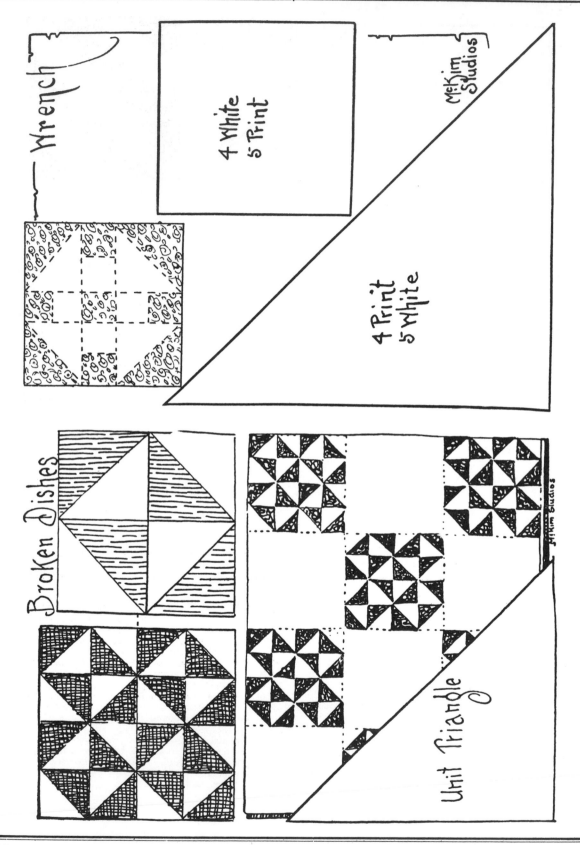

Wrench

McKim Studios

4 White
5 Print

4 Print
5 White

Broken Dishes

Unit Triangle

McKim Studios

1 Yellow
6 Orchid
12 Peach
18 Green
White for Paths

GRANDMOTHER'S FLOWER GARDEN QUILT OR THE FRENCH BOUQUET

THE lovely hexagon block quilts so popular at present are called by a variety of names and there are many ways of setting the hexagons together, too.

Hundreds of precise hexagons ready-cut means a real labor saving. If you are cutting your own, be careful to have one edge with the weave of the goods and all sides equal.

Seams are allowed on the unit hexagon pattern, although this may be larger or smaller to suit, just so the angles are the same and the six sides all equal. We have seen them only an inch across when finished, but a quilt of such small blocks is no temptation to the busy woman.

To make one block sew six orchid around 1 yellow center, 12 peach hexagons around this, then 18 green.

Straight seams may be run on the machine first, two orchid hexagons together, three groups of three peach, and six groups of three green. Then the other seams which fit in at an angle are best run by hand. A pillow is one such block, appliqued onto white.

Setting the hexagons together is most easily done by sewing three white hexagons on opposite ends of blocks which alternate with plain ones into a strip 4½ hexagons long. This will be about 63 inches or the width of the quilt center. Six such strips will finish about 76 inches long. A five-inch border of white all around augments this size to 73x86.

Yardage Estimate: Allow ¼ yard yellow, 1 yard orchid, 2 yards peach, 3 yards green, and 3¾ yards white.

WRENCH

THE wrench design is an authentic, old-time quilt pattern, and a very typical one, too. Simple to piece, adapted to the use of odd scraps, "dark and light," it still makes a charmingly conventional coverlet when carefully completed.

Patterns for parts do not allow for seams to make a 10-inch block. Blocks may be set into a quilt top either with alternate plain squares or lattice strips 2 inches wide plus seams.

If using print and white for the blocks, we suggest the lattice strip method using a plain tint for this which matches the print in color.

Materials Estimate: Three yards plain pink, for instance, with 3 yards each of

white and a pink print—9 yards in all —would make a pretty, full-sized quilt.

BROKEN DISHES

THIS is another example of charming quilts evolving from the simplest of cutting units. Here triangles are arranged into a sort of four patch as shown. Then four of these are four-patched together again into the broken dish block. These are all pieced exactly alike but turned at the different angle in alternate rows with the large plain white blocks between.

If seams are added the blocks will finish 11 inches square; if not, about 10 inches square.

This is an excellent pattern to select for using up odd bits of wash materials,

especially if the complete top is planned carefully, with the lighter tint blocks to the center, and blues, pinks, etc., so placed that they repeat a color and balance each other. Old-time quilt makers always "laid out" a top on the bed and thus figured the number of blocks, color placing and the complete size.

Material Estimate: Twenty-eight 11-inch pieced squares set together with 28 white blocks as in the diagram, 7 blocks wide by 8 long, finishes about 77x88 inches. It requires 3½ yards of white for the alternate plain blocks, 2½ yards of light and 2½ yards of dark for the pieced blocks, or a total of 8½ yards.

The Snowflakes quilting pattern would be particularly good on the plain squares that alternate with the pieced broken dishes.

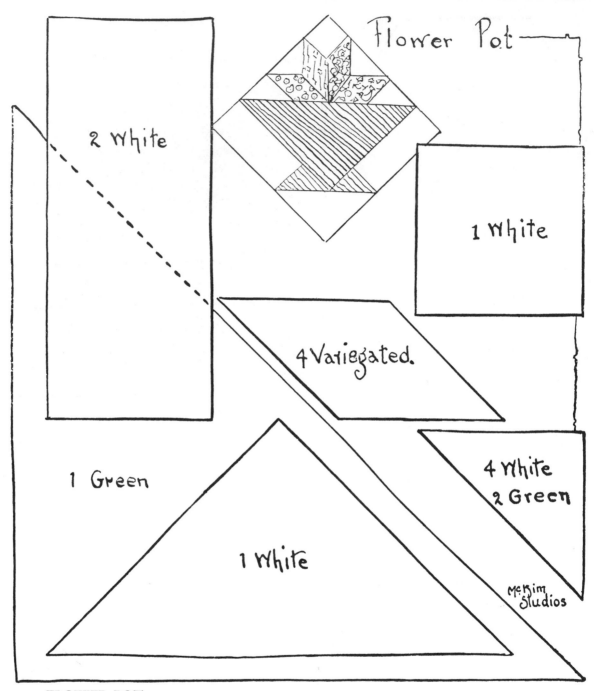

Flower Pot

2 White

1 White

4 Variegated.

1 Green

4 White
2 Green

1 White

McKim Studios

FLOWER POT

COULD you see a Flower Pot block pieced with its four gay diamond flowers in their angular pot you would instantly know the reason for this quilt's popularity. It is a charming block when made with a pink, blue, yellow and lavender print diamond all in a green pot with white background spaces. Or a still more modern effect of cactus may be obtained by using a terra cotta pot with alternate light and dark green diamonds on an unbleached background.

Add seams to the sizes here given for marking patterns and the block will finish about 7¾ inches square or 11 inches on the diagonal. If making a Flower Pot quilt, set the blocks together diagonally with alternate squares of white which may be quilted in a design made similar to the pieced blocks, or by using a Feather Circle or a Thistle.

Materials Estimate: Using 7 blocks wide by 8 blocks long, 56 pieced blocks. 42 plain blocks, 36 plain half blocks cut diagonally, and 4 plain fourth blocks for the corners will be needed. The finished quilt measures about 77x88 inches and requires 5 yards white, 2 yards variegated, 2½ green, or 9½ yards complete.

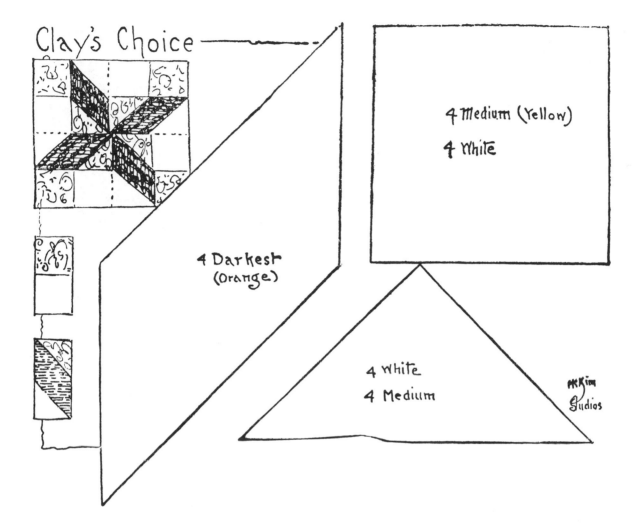

CLAY'S CHOICE OR STAR OF THE WEST

A QUILT pattern is ever so much more interesting if one knows its story. "Clay's Choice" is a very lovely block in its own right, but when it is traced back to the bitter Calhoun and Clay days one finds it as "Harry's Star," "Clay's Star," or "Clay's Choice" in the soft brown-tone prints of prewar days.

Then it becomes "Henry of the West" as the tide of empire surges Westward and another generation forgets Clay entirely and calls it "Star of the West."

"Clay's Choice" or "Star of the West" is easily pieced if developed as shown in the sketch. It might be set together with alternate plain squares of either white or yellow.

Materials Estimate: Blocks finish 10 inches square. Set together with alternate plain squares of either white or yellow it requires 36 pieced blocks, 36 plain blocks. This allows 8 blocks wide by 9 blocks long so that the quilt finishes about 80x90 inches. It requires 1½ yards of medium yellow, 1½ yards white, 1 yard orange and 4 yards of either medium yellow or white for the plain blocks. This is a total of 8 yards.

A Pineapple or Feather Circle would be effective for quilting pattern on the alternate plain blocks.

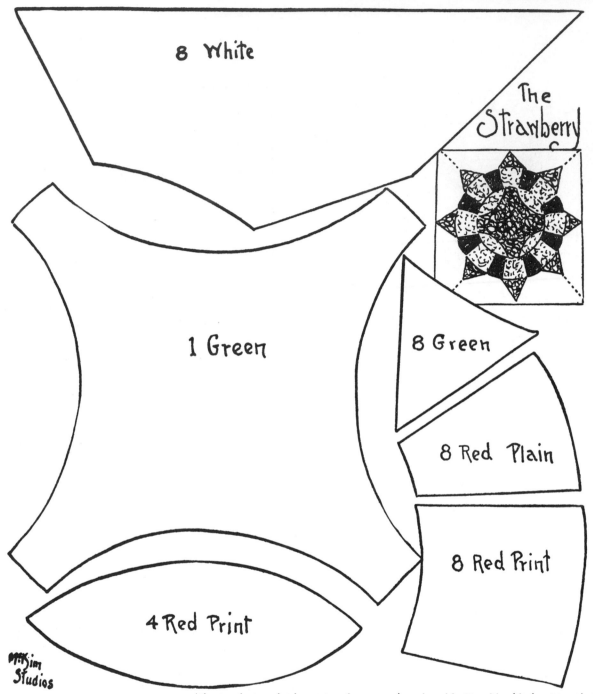

The Strawberry

8 White

1 Green

8 Green

8 Red Plain

8 Red Print

4 Red Print

McKim Studios

THE STRAWBERRY

THIS intricate block has another name less luscious than "Strawberry," but perhaps more colorful. It is sometimes called "Full Blown Tulip" and pieced with turkey red center, orange and lemon, set together on all green background it is gorgeous. Lattice strips instead of alternate squares make a beautiful all-over pattern when the top is completely set together.

The complete pieced circle with four corner triangles properly placed almost forms a square. Add to this the four outer strips each pieced of two odd white flanking a green triangle, and the block completes 12 inches square, or the pieced Strawberry may be appliqued onto a 13-inch square, disregarding the odd pieces marked "8 white."

Material Estimate: Twenty-one 12-inch pieced blocks set together alternately with 21 white blocks, 12 inches square, make a quilt 6 blocks wide by 7 blocks long and finishing about 72x 84 inches. This requires 1½ yards green, 1½ yards red print, ¾ yard plain red, and 6 yards white, or a total of 9¾ yards.

A quilting pattern exactly like the pieced block can be made by tracing the Strawberry design onto a brown paper, or use a 10-inch Feather Circle.

THE BUTTERFLY QUILT

HERE is an entirely new quilt that you will want — it's so dainty, different and altogether stunning. Twenty-one butterflies in prints and plain colors of yellow, pink and blue are all in one delightful, rainbow-hued scheme. Or, you may use scraps of prints for top wings and plain cloth for lower wings; all different would surely make a quite permissible plan for butterflies.

For the entire quilt 9 yards of material are required which includes the white for plain blocks, color prints and plain percales in all three tints, and boil-proof black for the bodies.

The Butterfly quilting design, shown on the quilted pillow in the sketch, would be lovely on the 21 alternate plain white blocks using a straight line lattice on the pieced ones.

THE TRUMPET VINE

THE Trumpet Vine is a very unusual design and makes up beautifully as you can see by the illustration. You will need eight and one-third yards of material for the quilt top.

As a quilting pattern to use on the alternate plain white blocks, we suggest the Vine design at the lower left of the illustration.

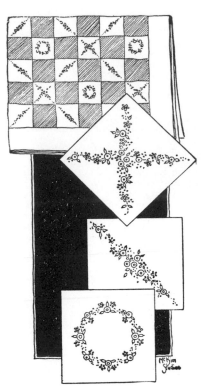

DRESDEN FLOWERS

SEVENTY-ONE little embroidered squares set together in a definite plan, alternating with plain ones to make a pattern which crosses itself in diagonal lines of flowers, centering every large square with a flower wreath, block, is suggested here.

Two color schemes are suggested—rose, pink, orchid, sky blue and green being one favorite, while coral, apricot, yellow, turquoise and green is another. In the first instance alternate blocks may be pink, orchid or blue, while yellow or green is recommended with the second grouping.

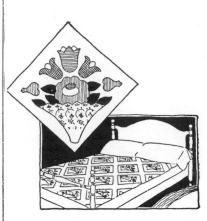

A CHARMING NOSEGAY QUILT

WE HAVE offered many quilt patterns, but never have we shown a gayer one than the Nosegay quilt. If you choose, you may carry out the lacy nosegay effect by using white embroidery material.

The embroidery or lace holder for the nosegay may be made in several ways. On the original quilt an eyelet embroidery about 6 inches wide was used. It takes 3 1-3 yards for the quilt.

For a full size quilt, 80 by 84 inches, the following material is required: 9 1-6 yards high grade percale, or 9 1-6 yards of finest sateen, assorted colors.

IRIS APPLIQUE QUILT

SOME like to piece, while others prefer applique, and then there's embroidery, but whatever your choice you should get the thrill of making a quilt.

The iris applique is assured of success because the design is so lovely, and yet it is not intricate to make. Orchid and deeper violet, two values of green, darker for the leaves and a bit of orange embroidery make the blocks. It is set together in an unusual manner with narrow strips of green and small orange squares at each intersection, alternate blocks plain to allow for fancy quilting.

A quilting pattern of a conventional iris spaces beautifully on the half and quarter blocks.

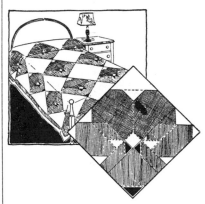

LET'S MAKE A PANSY QUILT

THE Pansy Quilt is pieced of lavender and violet with a bright little center in yellow and green. Sixteen pieced blocks with alternating white squares are enough for even a full sized quilt if borders are added as suggested in the small sketch.

THE HONEYMOON COTTAGE

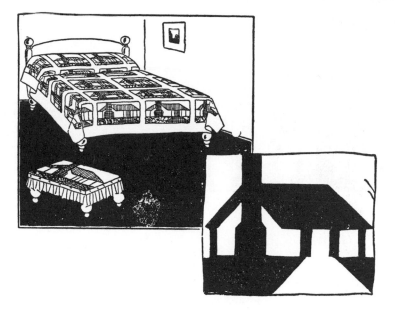

PATCHWORK has nothing to do with cross-patches, but as Mrs. Wiggs used to say, it is "keepin' the peace and doin' away with scraps." You'll love to do something pieced for the treasure chest, maybe several quilts that will be cherished for a generation or maybe just a precious "patchedy" pillow to start with.

The Honeymoon Cottage has a quaint old-fashioned charm that will appeal to all lovers of a squat, broad-eaved, little home with wide, hospitable doorway and fireplace. A block is simple to piece and when finished, measures about 12 by 15 inches. Twenty of the blocks set together with four-inch strips and six-inch border, make a quilt about 84 by 90 inches.

One block makes a clever pillow or stool top. A stool can be made at home by smoothly padding a board or shallow box and using wooden door stops, brass hooks, or large knobs, for legs. The edge finish for such a stool is a headed ruffle of green or any other color used in the pieced top.

BEAUTIFUL PANSY APPLIQUE AND QUILTED QUILT

THIS is an applique pattern using that gentle flower favorite, the pansy, conventionalized somewhat to form a center border which is really just twelve blocks, each 12 inches square. This is surely reducing the number of blocks in a quilt to a minimum, yet their close position on the quilt gives the effect of generous, even prodigal profusion.

This quilt is developed in the triad scheme—two tones of orchid, two of orange, and a soft green which also makes the center square, an outer band and binding with the remainder of white. The size of the finished quilt is 72 by 84 inches. Material assortment used in the original was 4½ yards of white, 2½ yards of green, and 1-3 yard each of the four other colors.

The quilting patterns suggested for making up this beautiful quilt include the center Feather Circle, 18 inches across, the Cable, Ostrich Plume, Feather Band, and Pineapple.

A BEAUTIFUL TULIP QUILT

THE tulip is simple to do and is attractive in yellow, orange and green or rose and orchid with green on a white ground. It sets together like a diamond paned window with white blocks and colored squares. This requires 20 blocks 10½x19, and 8½ yards assorted colors.

AN IRIS QUILT IS UNIQUE

THIS lovely iris makes up into a block about 14x17, so only 13 pieced blocks are used for the quilt. The blocks can be used to make a quilt or for the popular boxed pillows.

This quilt finishes 70x85 inches without border and requires 7¾ yards, six assorted colors.

MAKE A ROSE QUILT—OR PILLOW

THESE patterns piece a plump little rose in two values of pink with a yellow center, green leaves and applique stem. This stem curves over the alternating white blocks. Each block is 12½ square and the quilt finishes 80x88. It requires 8½ yards of five assorted colors.

Sunbeam Block

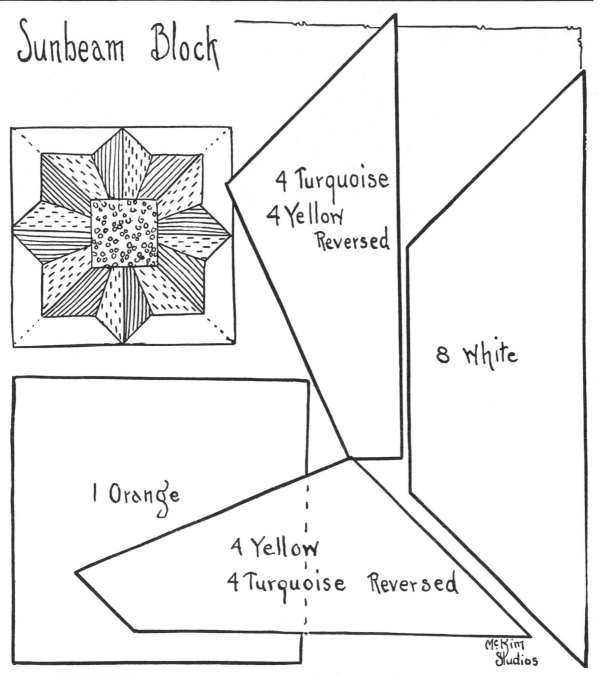

4 Turquoise
4 Yellow Reversed

8 White

1 Orange

4 Yellow
4 Turquoise Reversed

McKim Studios

SUNBEAM

TRANSFORMING sunbeams into a radiantly beautiful quilt is an achievement worth while. Even one little 12-inch pillow pieced in this pattern from gay silk or calico leftovers is acceptable, while a whole coverlet of sunbeams set together with alternate white blocks is most attractive indeed.

The four pieces which form each little fan which fits against the edge of center square sew together first. White edge blocks are then added, sewing onto the center square last.

Material estimate: A Sunbeam Block finishes 12 inches square which means about 17 inches diagonally. For a diagonally set plan, 25 pieced blocks alternate with 16 plain white, 16 half squares (triangles) and four quarter squares to make a quilt top about 85 inches square. You will need 1-3 yard orange, one yard yellow, one yard turquoise, 5 2-3 yards white. This is a total of 8 yards. One yard of orange additional makes a binding when cut into bias strips about 1½ inches wide.

Quilting suggestions: The pieced blocks are almost always quilted by following the lines of the piecing. On this design a similar plan, that is like the pieced sunbeam, looks well on the alternate plain blocks, or a ten-inch Feather Circle may be used.

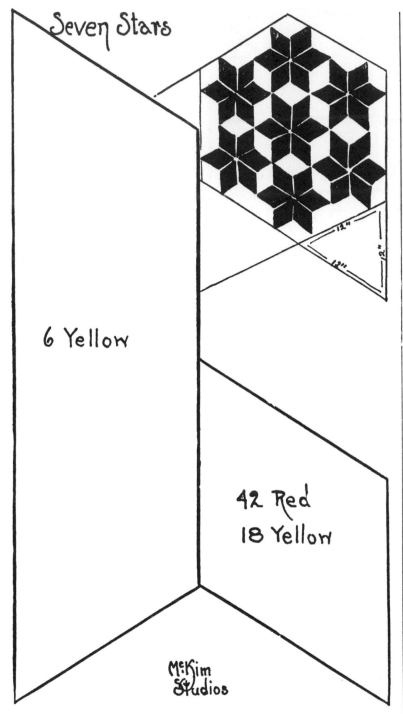

TULIP APPLIQUE

APPLIQUE is a form of patchwork more pretentious and extravagant than the good old-fashioned "piecing" variety. One layer of cloth, wholly for decoration, is applied to the background material with either blind or fancy stitching.

This broad, sturdy tulip in its bright red and green prints is one of the old time appliques and therefore is more artistic when made in oil calicoes and brown muslin fabrics. The background blocks should be about seventeen inches square. Seventeen appliqued blocks with eight plain are used in the small quilt design sketched.

Patches should be cut larger than the patterns here given to allow for seams. The small red print diamonds are creased under at the two top edges and basted to come under the large red diamond. The order is first to crease, baste, then blindstitch, and press.

Material estimate: Ten yards are required for making the Tulip Applique including green for the binding. 6½ yards white, 1½ yards red, ½ yard red print, 1½ yards green.

Quilting suggestions: The Conventionalized Rose and Bluebell would make a very satisfactory quilting pattern for this quilt. It is to be spaced twice into each block.

Cardboard patterns are made exactly like the ones here given. Draw around these onto material, but cut a seam larger and then sew back to the pencil line. As the Seven Star block is a good 20 inches across, and about 24 long, set together on all sides with the large yellow triangles, it only takes from 9 to 16 blocks depending on the size and borders wanted, to make a quilt. We cannot give exact cutting pattern for the large triangle here, but it is easily made this way: Mark an angle from your diamond block, extend 12 inches from each apex and connect. This should make equal angles and equal sides, about 11½ or 12 inches on each side.

Material estimate: Sixteen blocks without border finish about 86 by 96 inches. This requires 11½ yards: 6 yards red, 4½ yards yellow, and one yard of white for the inner diamonds.

Quilting suggestions: The Feather Circle, six inches in diameter, would make an interesting pattern for the large triangles.

SEVEN STARS

SEVEN STARS is a romantic sounding name, but the quilt really deserves this lofty title. It's a beauty, and the design formed by the 12 light diamond-shaped units within, is striking enough to warrant a third color.

For instance, use white for these, with the red and yellow prints suggested. This would mean 42 red diamonds, 12 white and only six yellow which sew in at the six outermost points of each block. Of course this is a rather difficult one to piece, as blocks sew in, rather than all going in straight seams.

Tulip Applique

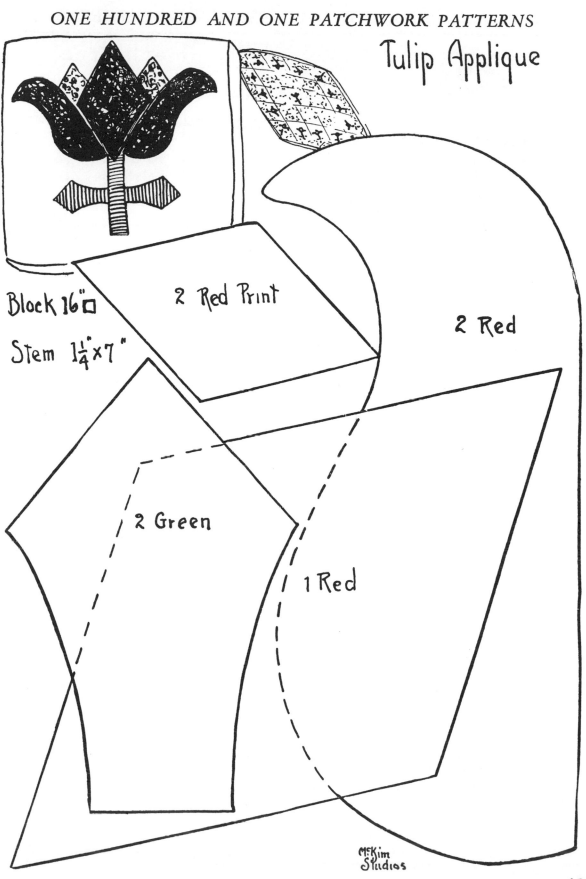

Block 16"□

Stem 1¼"×7"

2 Red Print

2 Red

2 Green

1 Red

McKim Studios

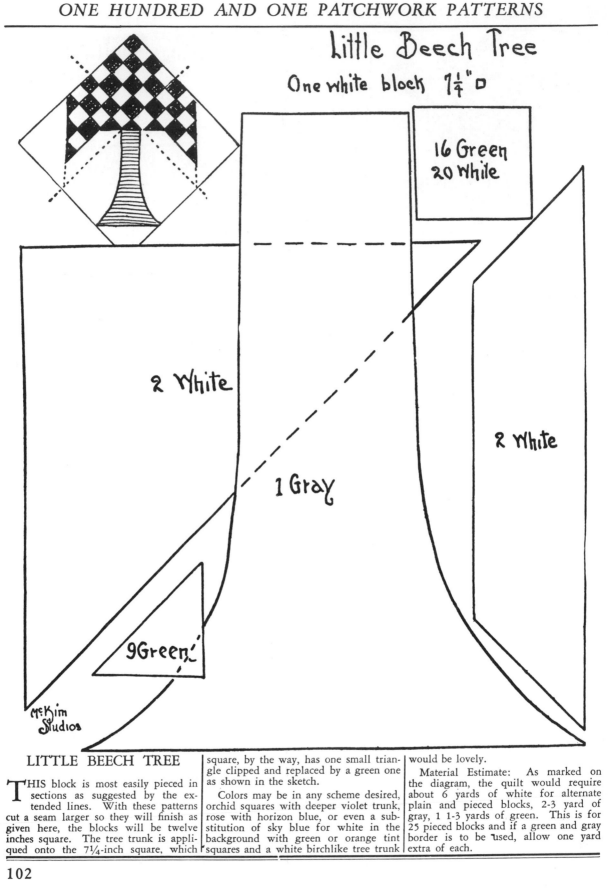

Little Beech Tree

One white block 7¼"□

16 Green
20 White

2 White

2 White

1 Gray

9 Green

McKim Studios

LITTLE BEECH TREE

THIS block is most easily pieced in sections as suggested by the extended lines. With these patterns cut a seam larger so they will finish as given here, the blocks will be twelve inches square. The tree trunk is appliqued onto the 7¼-inch square, which square, by the way, has one small triangle clipped and replaced by a green one as shown in the sketch.

Colors may be in any scheme desired, orchid squares with deeper violet trunk, rose with horizon blue, or even a substitution of sky blue for white in the background with green or orange tint squares and a white birchlike tree trunk would be lovely.

Material Estimate: As marked on the diagram, the quilt would require about 6 yards of white for alternate plain and pieced blocks, 2-3 yard of gray, 1 1-3 yards of green. This is for 25 pieced blocks and if a green and gray border is to be used, allow one yard extra of each.

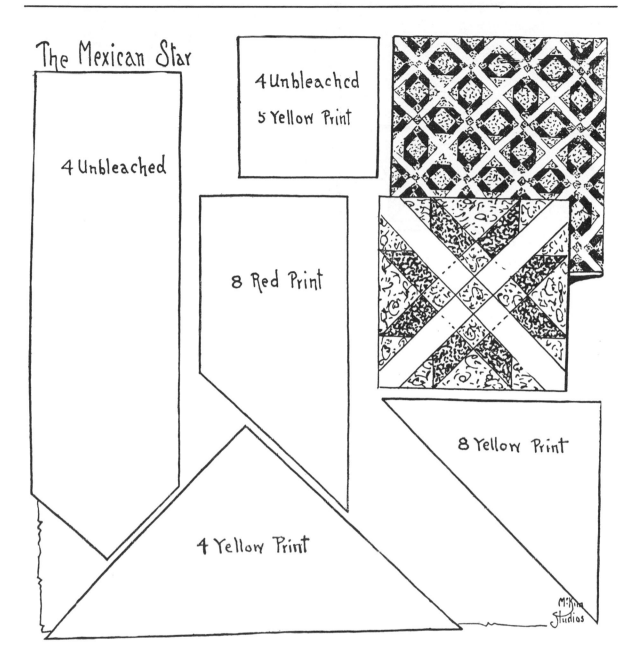

The Mexican Star

4 Unbleached

4 Unbleached
5 Yellow Print

8 Red Print

8 Yellow Print

4 Yellow Print

McKim Studios

THE MEXICAN STAR

RECENTLY a quilt collector found a beautiful old "Mexican Star" quilt up in the mountains of York State. It was a handsome specimen in reds and blues. How these same lovely patterns are found North, South, East and West testify of the far-flung ties that bound together the scattered settlers of Mexican War days, when this pattern was doubtless originated.

This is rather an intricate pattern to piece, but the effect when set together as shown entirely of pieced blocks looks more beautiful than bewildering. If you are a quilt enthusiast, "Mexican Star" will tempt you. Seams are not allowed.

A rather small center, with a band of unbleached, five or six inches wide, then a row of blocks and a final border of red or yellow makes a most interesting plan. Quilts are enriched by borders as pictures are by frames; and besides, this plain strip allows for a band of fancy quilting.

Material Estimate: The Mexican Star may be set together as shown in the sketch so the blocks make an all-over pattern. A finished block is about 10½ inches square. Made with 56 blocks, 7 blocks wide and 8 blocks long, a quilt will finish about 74 by 84 inches. This will require 3¼ yards unbleached, 2 yards of red print and 4¾ yards of yellow, ten yards in all.

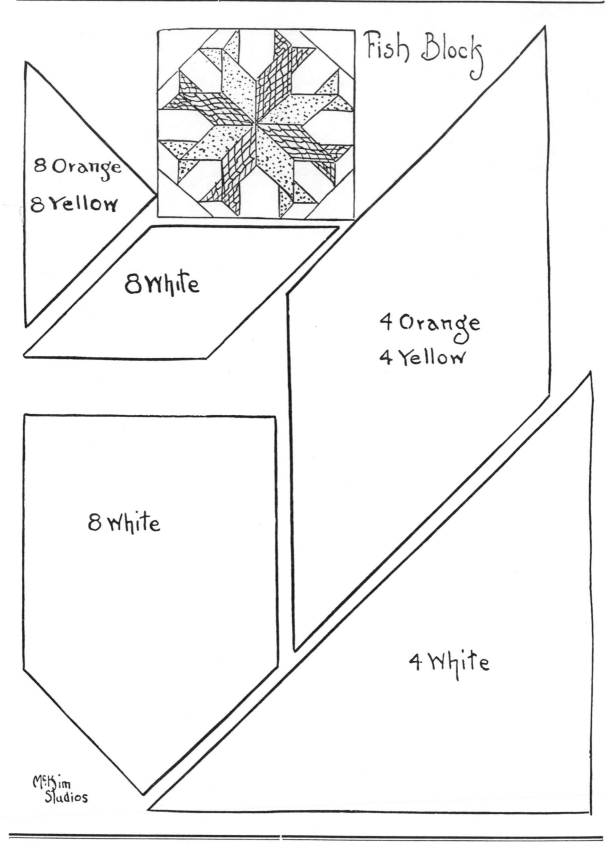

Fish Block

8 Orange
8 Yellow

8 White

4 Orange
4 Yellow

8 White

4 White

McKim Studios

THE FISH BLOCK

USUALLY it takes a splendid imagination to guess why our designing ancestors bestowed on their creations of squares and triangles such fanciful names. But here one can almost smell the salt water. Or if you have not the deep-sea eye for discovering marine life in calico, you still may appreciate in the Fish Block a most rhythmical and conventional design.

It finishes about 16 inches square if seams are added to the cutting patterns here given. These parts should be traced on cardboard or heavy blotting paper. Draw around them onto your cloth, keeping a true bias on all of these angle lines. Cut a seam larger and sew back to the marked line. This would make a most suitable quilt for a boy's room, seaside cottage, or really any room where the furnishings are "homey" enough to require a patchwork coverlet.

Material Estimate: Thirteen pieced blocks, put together with 12 alternate white blocks, and finished with three-inch borders of both orange and yellow, will make a quilt about 82 inches square. This requires 5 yards of white, 3 yards of orange, and 3 yards of yellow. To make the quilt longer than wide, add a four-inch strip of white at the top and bottom before adding the border.

Quilting suggestion: An Anchor design will add just the right flavor to this nautical design.

CORN AND BEANS

PERHAPS it was corn and beans time of year when this lovely old pattern was first made into a quilted coverlet. Or it may have taken its homely name from the golden corn color with green and unbleached which formed its color scheme. Any patchwork can be made of odd scraps, but the quilts of today are more apt to be planned as are all of our surroundings for exact harmony and smartness.

Cardboard patterns are cut exactly like the three triangles above; they trace onto material but cut a seam larger, as the patterns given are for the finished size to make into a block twelve inches square.

First piece four large triangles into a center square. Then piece four triangles B and add to form a larger square; then four blocks C, and finally the other four large white triangles.

For a cunning little chair cushion, omit these last four corners, leaving an octagon shaped block to pad slightly and quilt. To set together into a quilt, use alternate pieced and plain blocks, with either diagonal or vertical placing, only place them so the large center triangles follow across in consistent order.

Material Estimate: For the alternate plain block plan you will need about five yards of white, and two each of the colors. Lemon yellow with lettuce green would be dainty, or an apricot color with light blue-green, almost a turquoise tint. This is also a good scrap pattern using darker prints with light ones, or plain and designed cloth with a plain tint or white for each block.

Quilting suggestions: Feather Circle in the ten-inch size or Snowflakes would be suitable.

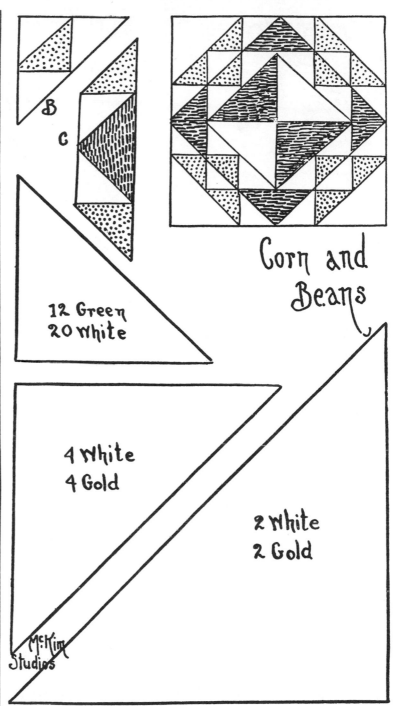

Corn and Beans

B
C

12 Green
20 White

4 White
4 Gold

2 White
2 Gold

McKim Studios

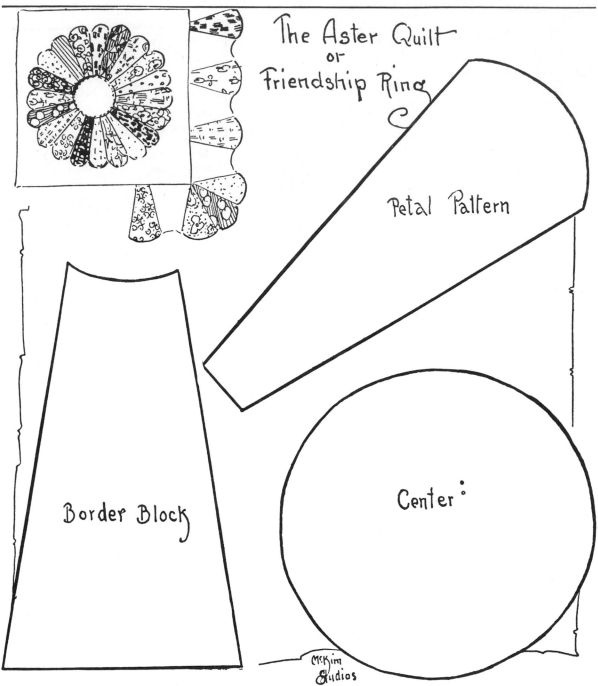

The Aster Quilt
or
Friendship Ring

Petal Pattern

Border Block

Center:

McKim Studios

ASTER OR FRIENDSHIP RING

ASTER, Friendship Ring, Dresden Plate, or whatever you call it, this quilt is certainly one of the prime favorites of today. Like the Wedding Ring, it uses as many variegated prints as can be assembled, hence the "Friendship Ring" part of its name as one usu-

ally has to call upon many friends for a proper assortment.

Sew the twenty petals together, then turn in around the outside scalloped edge and whip onto a fifteen-inch or larger background block of white or unbleached muslin.

The center circle whips down last to finish the block and then the white underneath may all be cut out if so desired. Twenty-five blocks make a full

size quilt, or twenty a twin size, with border as sketched, about 85 by 85 inches.

Material Estimate: Seams are not allowed, so cut enough larger than your pattern to allow for them. You will need 10 yards of material: 7 yards white or unbleached, and 3 of assorted prints—about 1-6 yard of each is the least one can buy.

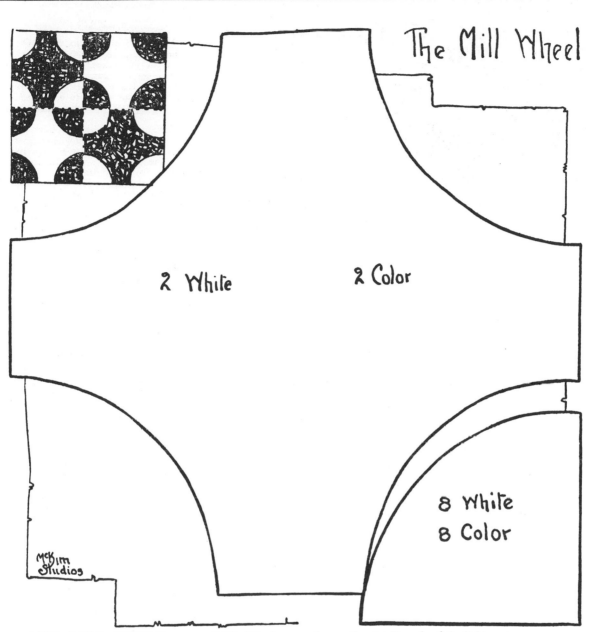

The Mill Wheel

2 White   2 Color

8 White
8 Color

McKim Studios

THE MILL WHEEL

THE QUILTS of the general Mill Wheel variety were exceedingly popular among old timers. In the "Base Ball" or "Boston Puzzle" only two corners were cut and filled in when the backgrounds were all dark and the four arc corners all light it was "Snow Ball." Watch your snip—only a few slight changes may produce the "Drunkard's Path" or a "Queen's Crown"!

Mill Wheel must have all pieced blocks to make a quilt top. As each block as sketched is 12 inches square, one can compute the number needed by the size she wants her finished spread. Allow seams extra and make all corners exact as any discrepancy will be noticeable when the wheels are fitted together.

Material Estimate: By using six of the 12-inch blocks across and seven down you will make a quilt about 72 by 84 inches. This will require 9 yards of material: 4½ yards dark and 4½ yards of the light.

More distinction for less work may be achieved by a smaller center, plain border of the light six inches wide, then a pieced border, then a plain border of the dark six inches wide, finishing the quilt any chosen dimensions.

Quilting suggestions: The Maple Leaf would be lovely on each large unit, or the Feather Rosette.

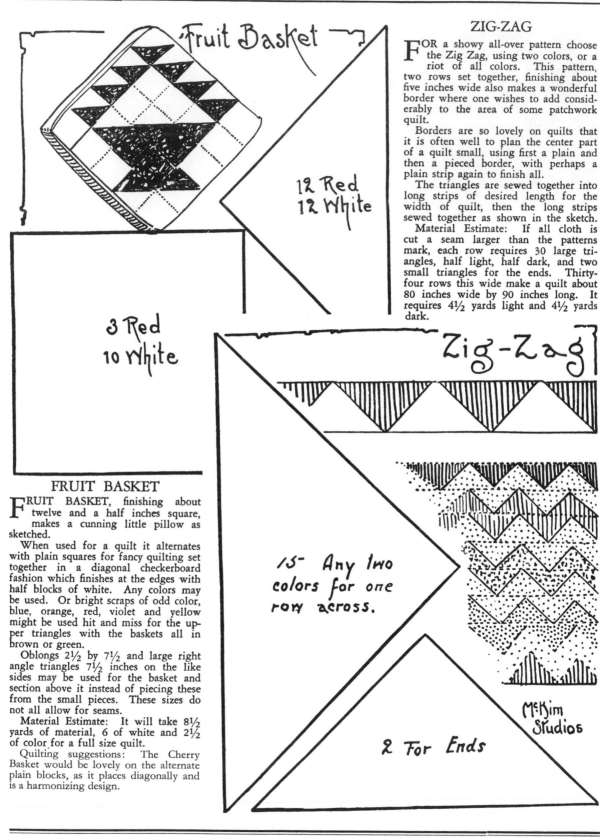

Fruit Basket

12 Red
12 White

3 Red
10 White

ZIG-ZAG

FOR a showy all-over pattern choose the Zig Zag, using two colors, or a riot of all colors. This pattern, two rows set together, finishing about five inches wide also makes a wonderful border where one wishes to add considerably to the area of some patchwork quilt.

Borders are so lovely on quilts that it is often well to plan the center part of a quilt small, using first a plain and then a pieced border, with perhaps a plain strip again to finish all.

The triangles are sewed together into long strips of desired length for the width of quilt, then the long strips sewed together as shown in the sketch.

Material Estimate: If all cloth is cut a seam larger than the patterns mark, each row requires 30 large triangles, half light, half dark, and two small triangles for the ends. Thirty-four rows this wide make a quilt about 80 inches wide by 90 inches long. It requires 4½ yards light and 4½ yards dark.

Zig-Zag

15 Any two colors for one row across.

2 For Ends

McKim Studios

FRUIT BASKET

FRUIT BASKET, finishing about twelve and a half inches square, makes a cunning little pillow as sketched.

When used for a quilt it alternates with plain squares for fancy quilting set together in a diagonal checkerboard fashion which finishes at the edges with half blocks of white. Any colors may be used. Or bright scraps of odd color, blue, orange, red, violet and yellow might be used hit and miss for the upper triangles with the baskets all in brown or green.

Oblongs 2½ by 7½ and large right angle triangles 7½ inches on the like sides may be used for the basket and section above it instead of piecing these from the small pieces. These sizes do not all allow for seams.

Material Estimate: It will take 8½ yards of material, 6 of white and 2½ of color for a full size quilt.

Quilting suggestions: The Cherry Basket would be lovely on the alternate plain blocks, as it places diagonally and is a harmonizing design.

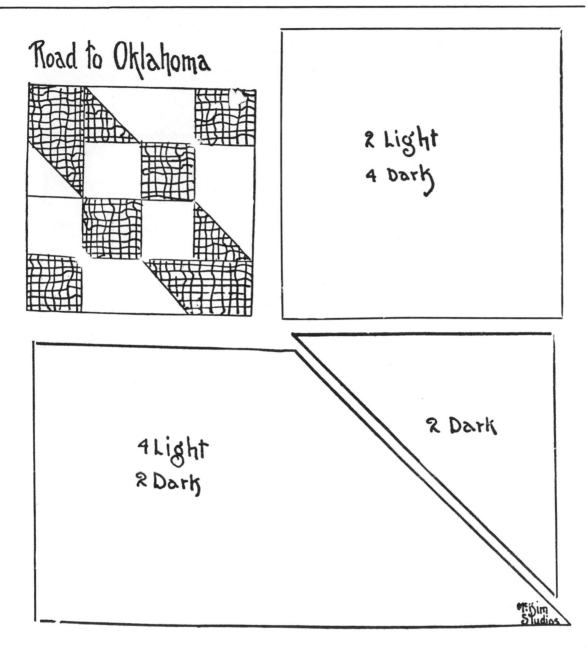

ROAD TO OKLAHOMA

SOME of our quilt followers ask for harder and more intricate patterns and some for something good looking that beginners can make. That's fair enough. Some of us never would attempt the "Rising Sun" or "Kaleidoscope."

"The Road to Oklahoma" is extremely simple to piece and it may be made of scrap materials. Yet when it is set together so that the little dark squares make a continuous path across the quilt, it is charming.

This quilt block some way suggests wings—well, why not, isn't the road to Oklahoma today an airway?

Blocks cut a seam larger to finish twelve inches square, or they may be the seam less and finish about ten and one-half inches.

Material Estimate: These blocks are 12 inches square and there are 42 blocks for the complete quilt, 21 pieced and 21 plain, which finishes about 72 or 84 inches. It requires 9 yards of materials, 6 of light and 3 of dark.

Quilting suggestions: Horn of Plenty is an unusual quilting pattern, or a Feather Circle 10 inches in diameter.

LOG CABIN

Here is a prime favorite of quilt makers for using silk scraps, and really for a slumber robe or fancy counterpane, a Log Cabin, properly shaded in light and dark is a thing worth cherishing. Old neckties, bits of sturdy ribbon, soft wool with silks and velvets, come into a glorified re-incarnation when cut into inch or inch and a half wide strips varying from one to nine, eleven or even thirteen inches in length, and sewed together as shown into blocks.

There is one center square of light, the very lightest, to two dark squares, each 2 inches longer than the one preceding, and the two longest ones of light to finish every block. Contrast between light and dark should be marked with the lightest values for the smaller pieces toward the center. Long dark strips may end with black each time, but should start with wine color, cinnamon brown or such.

This pattern gives the first four "Logs" in the Log Cabin block. To make a block 13 inches square as the small diagram indicates, extend the three additional light and two additional dark logs 2 inches in length each time.

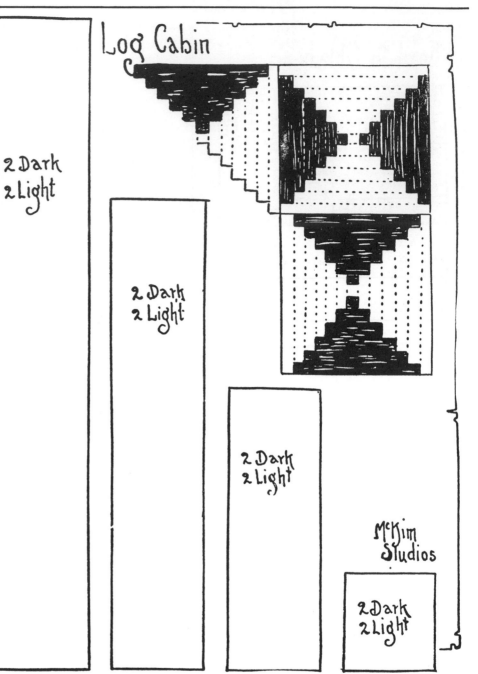

Another and perhaps more common way to build the "Logs" of color into blocks is to start with one square each of dark and light sewed together into a little oblong. Onto this sew a light oblong making a square. Onto this a dark oblong of the same size, 1x2, so that it goes across the end of the square formed by the little dark square and the end of the oblong.

From here on it is easy, alternating light and dark stripes of equal size but each pair one square longer than the pair before. These additions rotate around the center, right, bottom, left, top, right, etc., until a desired size block is built. The light finishes all across one side diagonally and the dark across the opposite.

Any Log Cabin quilt sets together entirely of pieced blocks, but there are at least four ways of doing this. After you have unit blocks completed it is well to experiment by laying them together for a plan you like best. With all dark corners—say at the upper right —so rows of dark and light triangles stair-step in even rows across the entire top, it is called "Straight Furrow."

A complete plan which backs four dark corners together for the quilt center, with a surrounding square of twelve turned in light ones, this having 20 dark halves around it, etc., is called the "Barn-Raising"—that is, if the whole is diagonally placed.

Where light alternates with dark in twos or fours, it is just Log Cabin, and all are lovely where the colors are rich.

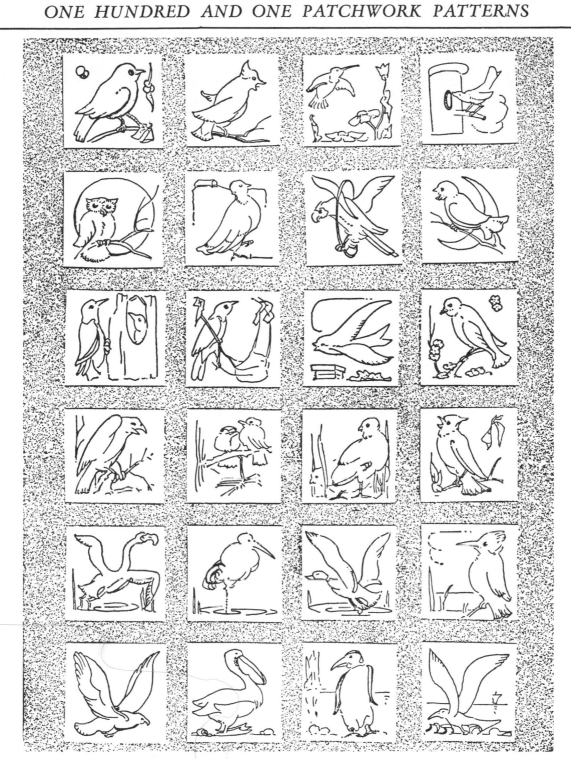

THE BIRD LIFE QUILT

STAMPED blocks are available today for many delightful quilts like the one suggested here, in which each of 24 bird friends is designed to fit a 9-inch square. You should have no difficulty in embroidering them; the work is mostly outline stitch with some wings and tails blanket-stitched to make a feathery edge. Fifteen skeins of thread in all colors would be needed to work the blocks. It requires seven yards for the quilt top and 2½ yards of 81-inch sheeting for lining.

DAISY CORNER

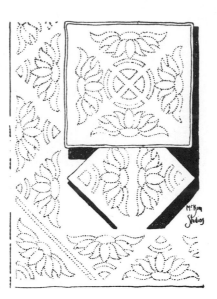

A PERFORATED pattern of proper quality may be placed wherever one wishes it, stamped, replaced and re-stamped a great number of times. The daisy corner is not a large pattern, only nine inches along its longer side, yet by combining it with itself it may be used on nine-inch squares or 12-inch squares as shown in the sketch, or repeated for a six-inch border with interesting corners.

EMBROIDERED FLOWER GARDEN QUILT

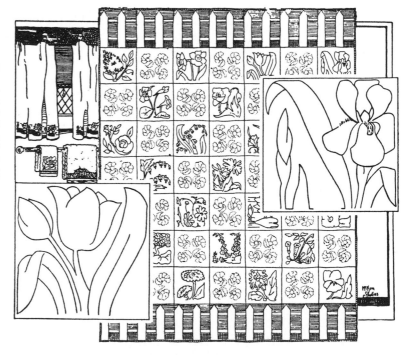

NOTHING makes a more intriguing set of embroidered quilt blocks than flowers. In this suggested design 25 stamped blocks 9 inches square alternate with 24 plain blocks of blue or any color to make a quilt top about 63 inches square. A nine-inch border, pieced or plain, brings the quilt size up to about 81 inches square or if you prefer a quilt longer than wide add wider plain color strips at the ends. The Four Flowers makes a lovely quilting design for nine-inch squares.

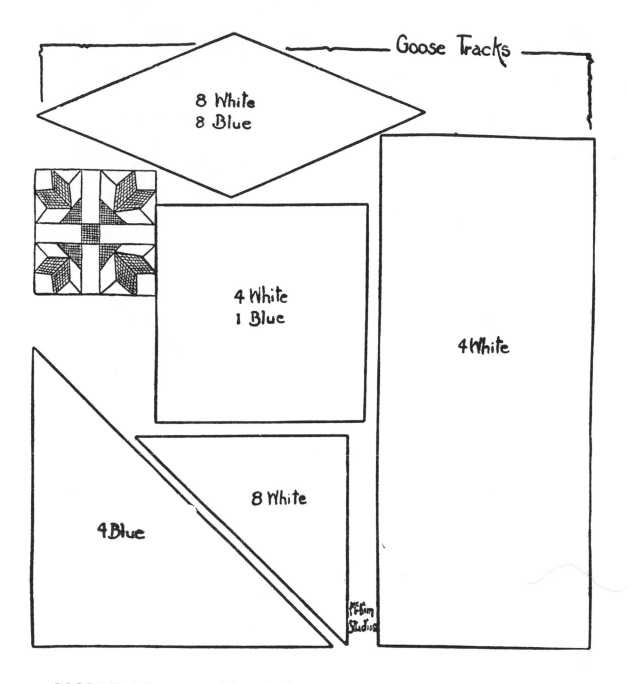

GOOSE TRACKS

IT IS interesting to note among the real old-fashioned blocks, the names and designs inspired by some track or foot print. There are Crow's Foot, Goose Tracks, Turkey Tracks, Bear's Paw, a lovely one called "Steps to the Altar" and the equally enchanting "Drunkard's Path." "Devil's Claws" is also a handsome block even when pieced of fiery red and white.

But to come back up to earth, Goose Tracks is really a charming old pattern, for either a two- or three-color combination. One follower of quilts sent in a sample of this block pieced in red, white and green which she called "Pride of Italy." The red was used for the diamond-shaped blocks with green for the square and 4 triangles marked blue.

Allow seams extra to the cutting sizes here given and a block will finish about 11 inches square. This quilt sets together with alternate white blocks, 6 blocks wide by 7 blocks long plus a 3-inch border and it finishes 72 by 83 inches. You will need 2¼ yards of blue material and 6½ yards of white.

The Snowflakes design or a ten-inch Feather Circle would be suitable to quilt on the alternate blocks.

Crossed Canoes

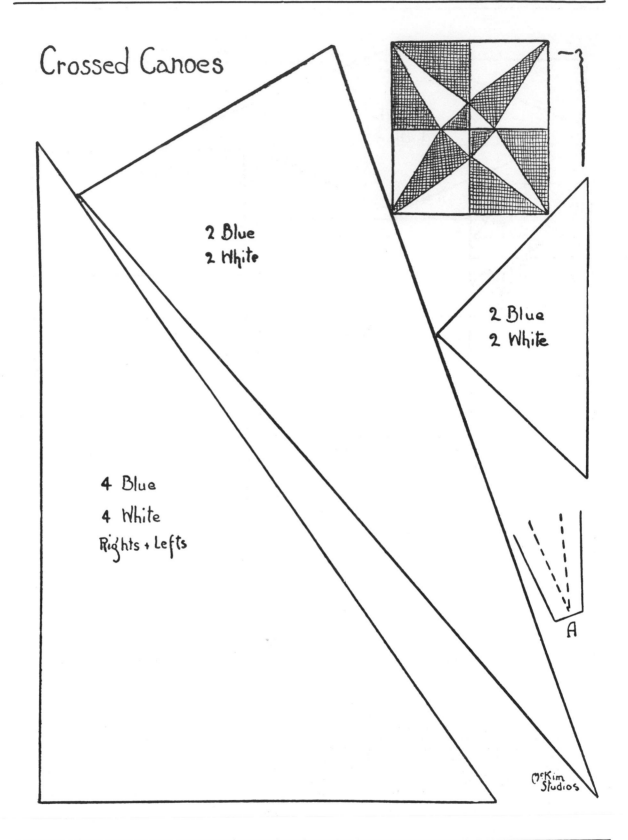

2 Blue
2 White

2 Blue
2 White

4 Blue
4 White
Rights + Lefts

A

McKim
Studios

BABY'S BLOCKS

THE Baby's Blocks patchwork has to be rather carefully pieced on account of the corners coming exactly together to produce that charming but puzzling geometric effect.

For a baby quilt in white, pink and rose, or three tints of blue this makes a cunning coverlet with edges left in points as it finishes, being then bound in the darkest of the tints.

As a quilt for the boy's bed it is quite masculine in unbleached, tan and red, different values of green or any scheme to harmonize with his room.

Equal amounts of three colors are used in this coverlet. We suggest for a full-size quilt 3 yards each of light, medium and dark. For a twin size, 2½ yards each of three colors and for a crib quilt, 1 yard of each color.

Quilting would be confined to very simple lines, such as follow the seams obliquely across in two directions would be practical and effective.

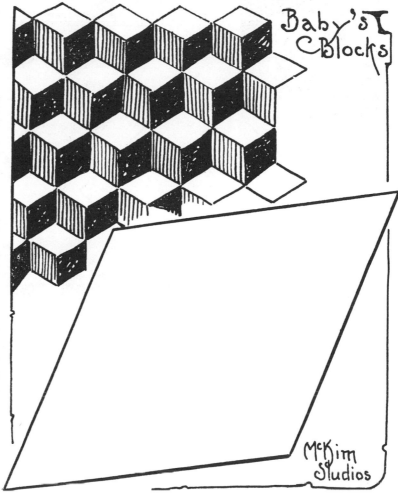

CROSSED CANOES

YOU will not be getting into very deep water if "Crossed Canoes" should be your selection for a quilt to try. There are only three seams to each quarter block as you can see by the small sketch, then the fourths sew together into a 14-inch square.

These blocks set together with white lattice strips about 3 inches wide with the dark boats pointing one way and the white ones forming an opposite diagonal pattern across the quilt. With a 3-inch border top and bottom, 25 blocks set together with 3-inch strips between will finish about 79 by 85 inches. A third color, red print for instance, could be used for the four dark triangles, leaving blue only on the four large parts here marked blue.

In cutting allow a seam all around in addition to the sizes here given. Diagram A shows how an acute angle is trimmed, rather than extend it away past the line marked by your cardboard pattern. This quilt will require 3½ yards of blue and 5½ yards of white.

An Anchor would be clever in design to quilt on the alternate blocks.

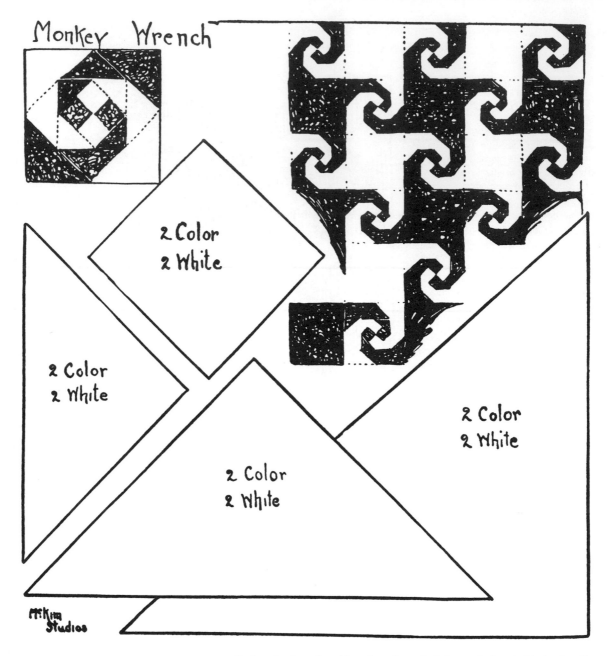

MONKEY WRENCH
OR SNAIL'S TRAIL

THIS stunning quilt is one of the best examples of how an exceedingly simple block may be set together into an intricate pattern. Pieced blocks of squares and triangles cut from the given patterns and pieced as shown, alternate with 10-inch plain blocks, dark in one row and light in another.

It really isn't hard to do, although each "monkey wrench" must be turned at a certain angle, one way in the row with large light squares and a turn further around in the next row with dark alternate squares.

Make cardboard cutting patterns of the four patterns here given. Mark around each with a lead pencil and cut a seam larger, sewing back to the pencil lines.

All blocks must be pieced exactly alike so they stack with light on light

and dark on dark. A block that "unwinds" backwards ruins the all-over pattern. The Monkey Wrench blocks finish 10 inches square. A top 70 by 80 inches plus a 2-inch border of each of the two colors, brings the size to 78 by 88 inches. You will need about 4½ yards of each color material for this size.

A Snowflakes design, Horn of Plenty, or Four Flowers would be right for quilting on the plain blocks.

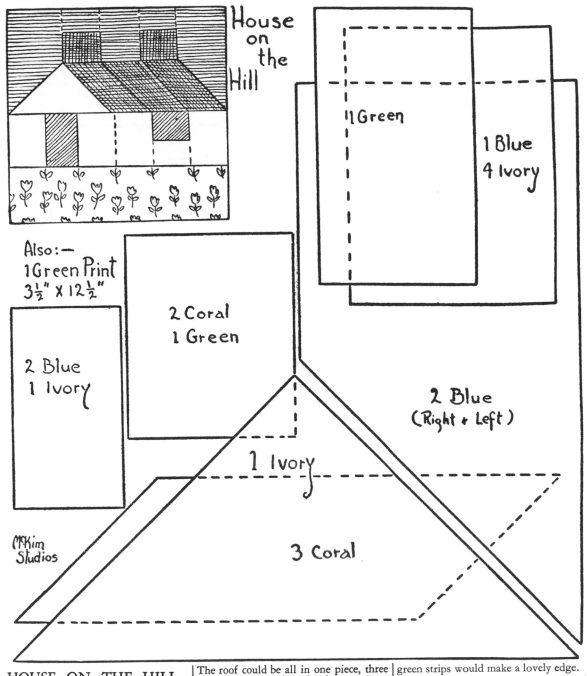

House
on
the
Hill

1 Green

1 Blue
4 Ivory

Also:—
1 Green Print
3½" X 12½"

2 Coral
1 Green

2 Blue
1 Ivory

2 Blue
(Right & Left)

1 Ivory

McKim
Studios

3 Coral

HOUSE ON THE HILL

MOST naturalistic of all the old-time quilt blocks are the House or Cabin patterns which piece with roof, chimney, windows, door, etc. You may have difficulty in distinguishing between a patchwork "Pineapple" and "Washington's Pavement," but House on the Hill really looks like that.

This is a cunning, dumpy little cottage with a variety of units, but very easy to piece once the materials are cut.

The roof could be all in one piece, three times the width of the block here given, but the smaller pieces with seams make it a bit more natural. The Hill block may be lighter green, plain or a flowered green print 3½ by 12½ inches.

All cloth is cut a seam larger than the patterns mark. The finished blocks should be set together with green or print lattice strips about 5 or 6 inches wide to place the houses apart in the quilt. A border with tulip corners would be right to quilt on these strips. Quite a wide border of ivory, blue, coral and green strips would make a lovely edge.

House on the Hill is a 12½-inch block and requires 20 blocks, 4 blocks wide by 5 long with 5-inch strips between and a 7-inch print border all around to finish 84 by 96 inches. You will need 1 yard of print, 1 yard blue, 1 yard coral, ½ yard green and 1¼ yards ivory. This 4¾ yards is for blocks only. Allow 4¾ yards extra of the print, blue or green, to set blocks together and make border.

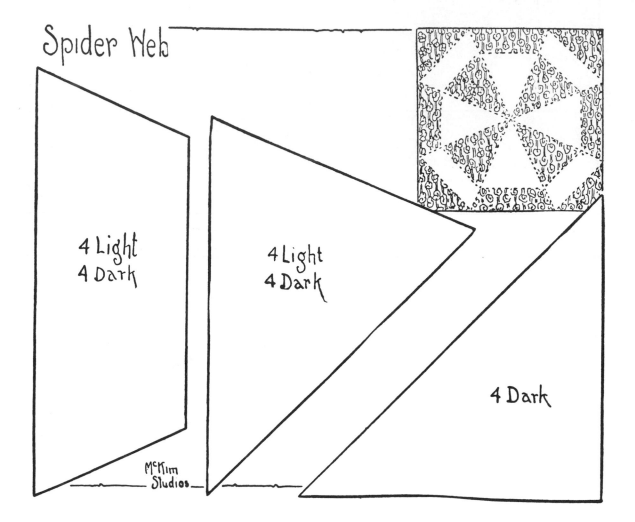

Spider Web

4 Light
4 Dark

4 Light
4 Dark

4 Dark

McKim
Studios

SPIDER WEB

SPIDER WEB blocks are rather particular piecing to make them lie perfectly flat when done. Most triangular pieces can be cut on a true bias with threads on two sides parallel with the weave of the material. But this, not being a right triangle, can not cut a true bias which means care must be taken to keep the long sides from stretching.

Piece the bases onto the long triangles first, then sew four pie-shaped pieces together for each half block. Put on the corner triangles, and sew one long seam through to complete.

For a full size quilt set together with white 11-inch squares, allow 5½ yards of white and 3 yards of a color. You will need 28 pieced blocks and 28 plain ones, or 7 blocks wide by 8 blocks long, making the quilt finish 77 by 88 inches.

For a twin size estimate the length of course is always the same, but the width may be planned any size from 63 inches to 78 inches depending on how much one wants it to hang over the sides, how deep the springs and mattress total, etc. For a Spider Web Quilt, twin size, you may use 6 blocks by 8, finishing 66 by 88 inches, which would require about 2½ yards of light color with 4¾ yards of dark.

The Wedding Ring Special quilting pattern could be easily adapted to quilt the spider web blocks, using the small flower for a border or lattice strips.

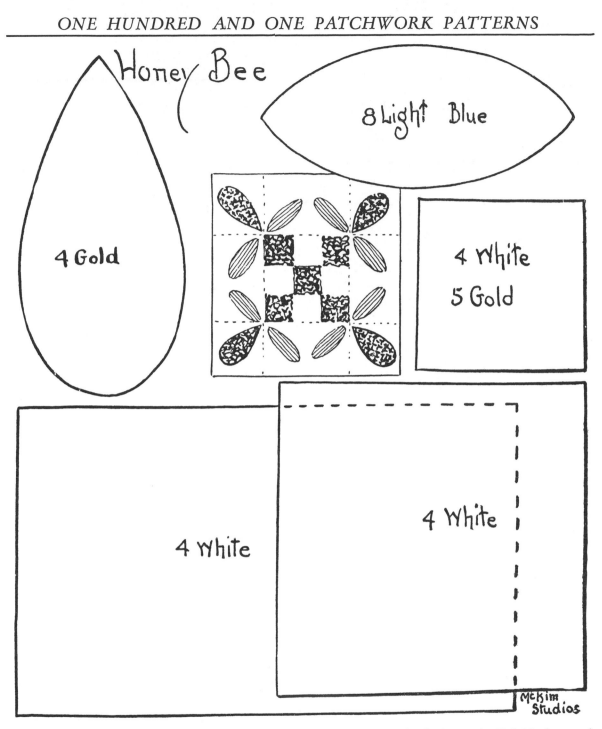

Honey Bee

8 Light Blue

4 Gold

4 White
5 Gold

4 White

4 White

McKim Studios

HONEY BEE

HERE is a charming example of a quilt design combining both piecing and applique. A little nine-patch block is used as the center block of another sort of nine-patch the other sections of which have applique as shown in the small sketch. These patterns may or may not allow for seams depending on the size you want the finished block.

It is a bit less ravelly to piece the entire block first and applique the bee's wings and bodies afterward. This is done by creasing a seam width back all around each piece, basting them carefully in place and then whipping or blind-stitching to the white background. Honey Bee blocks are much more attractive when set together with large plain white squares than just the one block suggests.

The quilt is 7 blocks wide by 8 blocks long and will finish about 77 by 88 inches. Or a smaller center with a 5-inch white border, appliqued with gold and blue "bees" would be unusual. This quilt will require 7 yards of white, 1½ yards of gold and ¾ of a yard of light blue.

The Snowflakes or a ten-inch Feather Circle would be effective on the odd blocks.

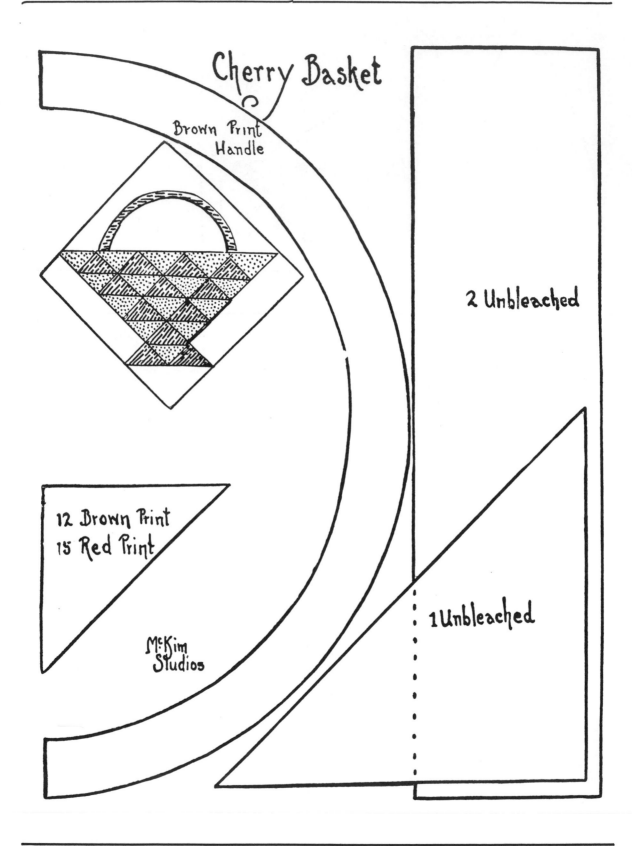

Cherry Basket

Brown Print Handle

2 Unbleached

12 Brown Print
15 Red Print

McKim Studios

1 Unbleached

CHURN DASH

THE CHURN DASH is only another variety of nine-patch, one with a name that looks very like the object specified.

These patterns make a block 9 inches square if seams are allowed additional to the units here given. Odd scraps may be used for the different blocks, especially when set together in some definite order. Lightest prints to the center shading to the darkest in the outer rows gives a plan to the whole. With lattice strips of some one color about 2 inches finished, the churn dash makes a clever coverlet.

This quilt, 7 blocks wide by 8 blocks long, will finish about 75 by 86 inches. You will need 3 yards of white, and 5½ yards of print would be used if the block set together with print strips. If set together with alternate white squares, these amounts would reverse, 3 of print and 5½ of white.

With this plan one might use Horn of Plenty to quilt on the alternate squares or the Four Flowers.

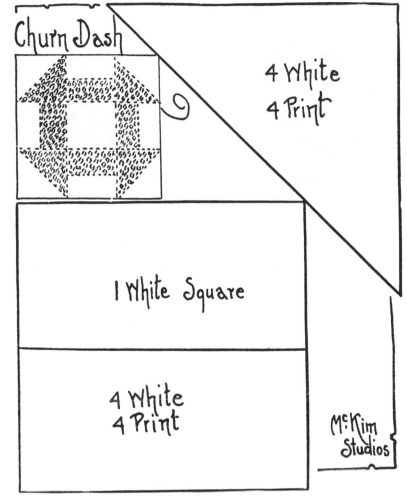

CHURN DASH

4 White
4 Print

1 White Square

4 White
4 Print

McKim Studios

CHERRY BASKET

IN THE Cherry Basket we have a pattern that requires only half of the blocks pieced. It sets together always with alternating squares on the diagonal, filling in at the four sides of the quilt with white half-blocks to complete. There are several basket versions but this one with appliqued handle and pieced basket is particularly effective. It makes a block 12 inches square, patterns for all parts being here given except the large triangle upon which the handle is appliqued. This is easily cut by taking any paper at a right angle, measuring 10 inches down each side and drawing across.

Make your set of cardboard patterns exactly like the ones here given. These do not allow for seams; draw on the cloth around cardboard, but cut a seam larger and then sew back to the pencil line. Cherry Basket makes a good number to select for one of those popular patchwork pillows, as well as for a Colonial quilt. It takes 25 pieced blocks, 16 plain blocks, and 16 plain half blocks cut on the diagonal for sides, also 4 plain one fourth blocks cut on the diagonal for the corners. Allow 6 yards of unbleached, 2 yards of brown print and 1½ yards of red print.

The Cherry Basket quilting pattern is especially designed to go with this block.

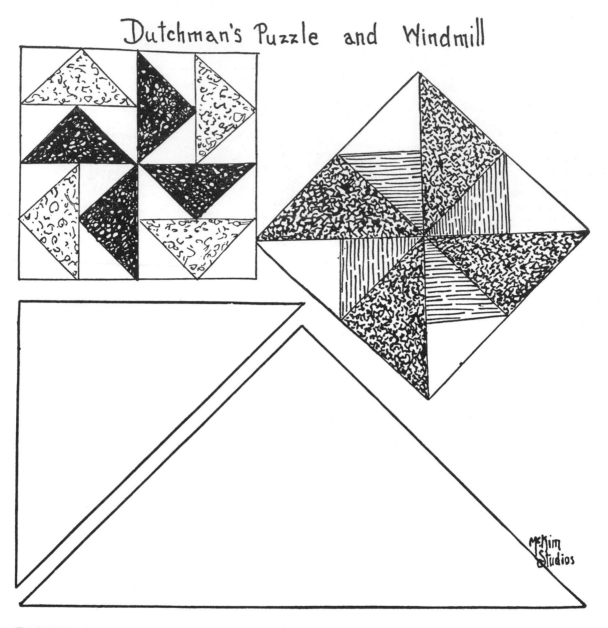

Dutchman's Puzzle and Windmill

DUTCHMAN'S PUZZLE AND WINDMILL

THE two triangles on this page are the basis of a "double header" number with no additional charge for admission! In two clever ways it proves what can be done with a pair of triangles, one, half the area of the other, by using white and two colors.

In Dutchman's Puzzle two smaller triangles add to a larger about like the cutting chart patterns are placed, and this twice done forms a square, ¼ of the finished block. The darker always points into the lighter and thus the Puzzle is solved into a 12-inch block.

Windmill is quite a different arrangement, even more simple which makes a block 8½ inches square.

A windmill quilt 85 inches square takes 100 8½-inch blocks, 50 of them plain and 50 pieced. Allow 4¾ yards of white, 1 yard light blue and 1¾ yards dark blue, or 7½ yards of material.

Dutchman's Puzzle, on the upper left, can be made of red print, yellow print and unbleached muslin, making the 4 large center triangles red print, the four large outer triangles yellow print and the 16 small triangles of the unbleached. There will be 28 pieced blocks and 28 plain blocks, making a quilt 84 by 96 inches, or 7 blocks wide by 8 blocks long. A quilt of this size requires 1¼ yards red print, 1¼ yards yellow print and 6½ yards unbleached muslin.

Six-inch Feather Circle or the Thistle would be right size for the Windmill block, while the Snowflakes or a 10-inch Feather Circle would fit the Dutchman's Puzzle.

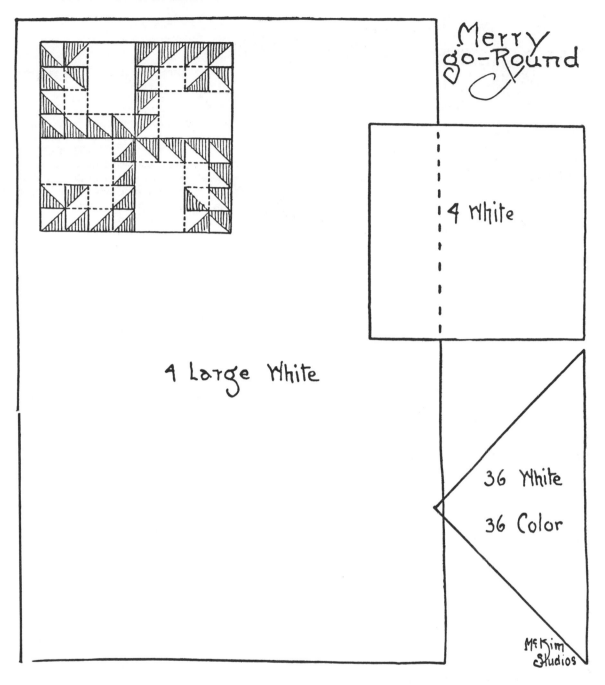

Merry go-Round

4 White

4 Large White

36 White

36 Color

McKim Studios

MERRY GO ROUND

THIS is an admirable design for using odd scraps of bright wash goods; each block may be a different color so long as the light and dark value remains about the same. The thing that makes so many old quilts disreputable looking is a few really dark blocks, navy blue, or lead colored percale, irregularly spaced and showing up like great holes in an otherwise light colored pattern of pinks, yellow and pale blue. There must be a plan for the whole quilt when using scrab bag pieces.

These cutting units may or may not be cut a seam larger than the sizes here given. The Merry Go Round block as shown is really four blocks all exactly alike. By using these units and allowing for a seam, 9 pieced blocks 18 inches square will be needed. Set together with 18 strips cut to finish 4½ by 18 inches. Fill in the square at the end of these strips with a 4½-inch pin wheel like the unit in the center of the block. Eight of these small squares will be needed. Put the 4½-inch strip at each end, but not on the sides of the quilt, to add length. This makes a finished quilt about 85 inches wide by 94 inches long; requires 6½ yards white with 2½ yards of colored material.

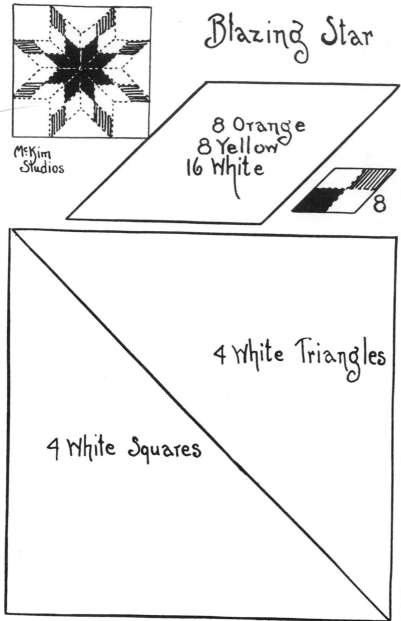

Blazing Star

McKim Studios

8 Orange
8 Yellow
16 White

8

4 White Triangles

4 White Squares

BLAZING STAR

THERE are ever so many quilt patterns but none are more charming than this shaded eight-point one often called the Blazing Star. Eight little diamond-shaped four patches are pieced and set together with background triangles to form the block.

Any grouping of colors may be used, and a third color, as lighter yellow or pale green with the above plan of yellow and orange could be used instead of the white diamonds. With seams added to the cutting patterns here given the block finishes about 13½ inches square, or without seams added, 12 to 12½ inches.

This quilt sets together with alternate plain blocks, and includes 21 pieced blocks, 21 plain blocks and is 6 blocks wide by 7 blocks long plus a 2-inch border which makes it finish about 80 by 93 inches. It requires 1 yard orange, 1 yard yellow and 6½ yards of white. Allow one yard extra of orange for the border.

THE QUILT'S LINING

THE LINING is quite important. It must be soft, without starch filling, and should match the texture of the pieced top as nearly as possible, as a soft sateen lining with sateen top. For wide quilts allow 3 widths of 36-inch material, having the center one full width and tearing equal parts off of the outer two, or using two full widths with a narrow center strip.

There is an excellent soft sheeting woven especially for quilt linings in white. Two and a half yards is ample for most quilts.

Colored sheeting is sometimes used for quilt linings also, but it comes in a heavier weight. Colored 81-inch sheeting is a good background for quilt tops where a large central applique plan is used or for such designs as the Rose of Sharon, Hollyhock Wreath, or Tulip applique.

Colored linings in some repeat tint from the quilt top are justly popular, and in some ways more practical than white linings.

YARDAGE ESTIMATES

WE HAVE had yardage estimated for the hundred and one patchwork patterns in this book. Should you wish to know how much material to buy for some other patterns, the method is this: Take one block, and make a tracing of each part the number of times it appears in that block. Estimate the area covered; for instance, there are 6 blue triangles of one size and 4 blue squares in a block with white and a print. The six blue triangles take a space say 4 by 12 and the squares 4 by 16. This will total 4 by 28. There are 18 blocks in the quilt—4 inches will cut 9 times out of 36-inch width—two times 28 is 56 inches so we will allow at least 60 inches or 1 2-3 yards of blue. They will not always figure out to perfect advantage, using every inch, so be are often difficult to match later.

THE STANDARD BOOK OF QUILT MAKING AND COLLECTING
by Marguerite Ickis

Here is the best available book on quilt making—a complete, easy-to-follow guide that shows you how to make beautiful, useful quilts that you will be proud to own and display. Even if you are a beginner, you will soon find yourself quilting like an expert, by following these clearly drawn patterns, photographs, and step-by-step instructions.

All the information you need is here, lucidly and thoroughly explained. You learn how to plan the quilt, the number of blocks to fit a bed, how to select the pattern to harmonize with the design and color of the room, and how to choose materials. You are told how to cut, sew, make appliquéd patterns, patchwork and strips. An entire chapter on design discusses basic elements, sources, making your own designs, avoiding sewing problems, how to use the rag bag, and much more, while the section on patterns gives directions on tracing, seam allowance, and estimating quantity. There is full information on borders, quilting and tufting, and just about every other aspect of quilt making.

Mrs. Ickis shows you over 200 traditional and unusual quilts, including Basket, Tree of Life, Flowers in a Pot, Traditional Geometric, Friendship, Square and Cross, Saw Tooth, Drunkard's Path, Flying Geese, Mexican Cross, Pennsylvania Dutch, Crazy Quilts, Yo-yo Quilts, Album Quilts, and dozens of others, including over 40 full size patterns. You are given other uses for quilting, such as drapes, curtains, upholstery, lunch cloths, purses, cushions, and Italian quilting.

Completing the coverage are fascinating chapters on collecting quilts as a hobby; how to make full-size patterns of famous American quilts from pictures, small designs, and museum or collector's quilts; and an historical story of quilt making, with personal memories.

Index. 483 illustrations. One color plate. xi + 276pp. 6¾ x 9½. T552   **Paperbound $3.00**

From Sunset Quilting & Patchwork

Needles:
  Sewing + quilting: No7 - No10 for
    small even stitches
  milliners' No3 - No9 needle is long
    + sharp for appliqué work

Best filling is dacron batting.
  Old blankets + mattress pads too
    heavy
  Cotton batting hard to sew,
    lumps when washed.

Mattresses:
    crib 27" x 48"
    twin: 39 x 75
    double 54 x 75
    queen 60 x 75
    King 72 x 84"

Bed spreads: reach floor, + 20"
        to cover pillows
  coverlets: add a few inches
    all around matts. size to allow
    for quilting and person sleeping
    beneath it

a throw or carrobe: 4' x 6'

Add 4-6" all around for hems +
seams.

Press seams flat - NOT OPEN

Tying a quilt (instead of quilting)
  in a grid (every 4")
  or in a pattern.
  -Don't use cotton

Pin- baste entire quilt on floor

Use long sharp yarn needle +
  2yds yarn or floss, doubling it.

Do not knot yarn
Square knot

For hot mats use
cotton batting or
mattress pads or
old blankets. (Dacron
conducts heat).